D1625139

The
Restart
Roadmap

JASON TARTICK

The
Restart
Roadmap

Rewire and Reset
Your Career

HarperCollins
LEADERSHIP

AN IMPRINT OF HarperCollins

Published by HarperCollins Leadership, an imprint of HarperCollins Focus LLC.

Any internet addresses, phone numbers, or company or product information printed in this book are offered as a resource and are not intended in any way to be or to imply an endorsement by HarperCollins Leadership, nor does Harper-Collins Leadership vouch for the existence, content, or services of these sites, phone numbers, companies, or products beyond the life of this book.

Book design by Aubrey Khan, Neuwirth & Associates.

ISBN 978-1-4002-2687-0 (eBook)
ISBN 978-1-4002-2686-3 (HC)

Library of Congress Control Number: 2021951961

Printed in the United States of America
22 23 24 25 26 LSC 10 9 8 7 6 5 4 3 2 1

FOR MOMMA CALUCH & GAR-BONE,
thank you for the consistent support, love, and encouragement through each and every day, since day one . . .

CONTENTS

The
Restart
Roadmap

1

The Sunday Night Scaries

I am on the floor of a well-appointed executive men's bathroom at the headquarters of an important client. At the moment, I am having a flat-out, full-featured anxiety attack—trembling, sweating, turning white as a ghost, hugging myself for dear life, absolutely terrified. Beads of anxiety-propelled sweat are dripping off my forehead and stinging my eyes. Sweat is coursing down my spine and soaking my Brooks Brothers shirt, the one I had to have but waited to buy till Black Friday. I am totaled.

I was at the client's headquarters as part of my rapid rise up the corporate ladder, where I was perceived as someone on the fast track. Specifically, I had been asked to accompany a senior banker to an important client meeting. His name is William; he prefers going by "Bill."

Actually, the meeting was more like a cattle auction. An important piece of business was at stake, and just about every bank in the area was pitching its own plan for it.

The pitch took place in a long, long conference room. The CEO of the company was at the head of the table, the chief financial officer was at his side, and a lot of other obviously high-level execs were seated—in descending order of title, no doubt—down the table on either side. Everyone in the room, both the banker pitchers and the client catchers, knew exactly what was going on and how high the stakes were.

Our game plan was that Bill would make the presentation and do all the talking. I was there to represent the brand. My job that day was to look right, to say the right things without ever getting a single fact wrong and without ever stumbling over a single word, and to assume the proper posture, just as I had done many times in the past. I was a "message." My presence told the client's team that our bank not only had depth of talent, but we also kept an eye on the future, represented by yours truly, a twentysomething up-and-comer. I helped convey the message that we were a smart, forward-looking bank that knew how to make our clients feel like they were our highest priority. That there were just the two of us representing our bank shows you just how much trust was being placed in me to get it right. And to act composed and correct while doing it.

So, senior banker Bill and junior banker me faced off against the dozen or so client execs in position around the table. Bill signaled for the first PowerPoint slide, and our pitch was underway. All eyes were riveted on the screen, all ears attuned to Bill's smooth presentation, and I was right there, in the role—until suddenly, I felt my chest tighten and my heartbeat speed up something crazy, and somehow, I just knew that I had to get the hell out of there. It was, quite simply, the basic fight-or-flight response kicking in.

"Excuse me," I said, and all eyes turned to me. "Is there a bathroom?" Bill shot me a look: *What are you doing? Are you nuts?!? Hold it in!*—but one of the client execs replied that it was "just around the corner," and I bolted, hoping that I did not look as bloodless as I felt.

I found the place, locked the door behind me, and that's when I fell on the floor. I really don't know how long the anxiety attack lasted until I managed to pull myself back together and head back into the meeting. Senior banker Bill seemed mollified. Apparently, I really had looked awful. But the presentation had gone well. What I mostly remember is that when he and I left the meeting and walked outside to our cars, I took in the sweetest breath of fresh air I had ever known.

Even before that anxiety attack, I had begun to realize that the life I was living wasn't the life I had planned, and it sure as hell wasn't the life I wanted.

The exact moment is a little blurry, but the realization was crystal clear: I felt like I was in career jail Monday to Friday. Those five days, I followed a script: show up early, stay late, work hard, dress appropriately, look the part, act the part, always say yes, live by the company mission . . . blah . . . blah . . . fucking blah!

Till late Friday afternoon, when the cuffs came off and I found myself at the bar in town ordering shot number one and "Keep 'em coming!" I took that first sip, held it in my mouth for a second, swallowed, coughed slightly because I suck at shots, but even with that, it was the first time in five days that I felt free.

Yet by Sunday afternoon I was feeling jumpy all over again, and by Sunday night I was way down, flattened by my own personal kryptonite, the "Sunday Night Scaries." That's what I called the sharp, jittery stabs of stress that seemed to eat away at my gut because of what was coming up the next day.

And when I heard the office door close behind me Monday morning, I felt locked in all over again with the walls closing in on me.

And here's the thing: I felt this way despite the fact that I had the job I had wanted and planned for pretty much since I could remember. I got that job right out of college, where I had earned a bachelor's degree in business administration. I was hired by a highly regarded financial corporation seen as innovative and growing, and I was assigned immediately to its elite management training program. And by the time I started wondering what the hell I was doing there, I was already a corporate-banking relationship manager scoring off-the-charts performance reviews and moving swiftly up the ladder of success. In other words, I was just where I was supposed to be in my career plan—maybe even a little ahead of the plan—and all I wanted was to get out.

Do you ever feel the way I did? Because I know I'm not alone in this.

A lot of my colleagues at the bank grumbled along with me about the corporate "culture" and all that came with it. Yes, we shared pretty much the same expectations of climbing up the ladder title by title, promotion by promotion, raise by raise—grinding it out year after year—and we were clear-eyed, or so we thought, about what that ascent would take out of us. We all hated it but joked about how we had to "look the part," fit into the image the execs called "leadership," dress in a way that "reflected the company's culture," and maintain the impression that we were always striving upward.

Well, we *were* always striving upward, but that's because you couldn't get away from the pressure to at least always *look like* you were striving upward. The message was issued nonstop, if perhaps subconsciously, from the top. We were constantly being made aware of those just a bit above us who were "making it" big-time. We knew that senior management called them the Hi-Po Group, the "high-potential" people who seemed to have a rocket on their backs propelling them to the top. I just thought they were batshit-crazy-out-of-their-minds-obsessive. But the nickname kept us Hi-Po wannabes drinking the Kool-Aid.

And the truth is that I kind of believed it. I wanted to be part of it. What senior management was telling us, in a strategically passive-aggressive way, was that we either found a way into this group or we ended up status quo. Hi-Po Group or Bust, boys and girls! You either make it into that in-group, or you will be a passed-over nobody stuck at midlevel for the rest of your career. So, yes, I bought the Hi-Po Group concept—hook, line, and sinker— and so did all of my peers. Tell me what to do, how to do it, where to live, and how to live it . . . I am in. I swear I am not talking about a cult; I refer to what is literally just the well-oiled machine grinding away in a large bank—and grinding you down as well.

It wasn't a stretch to think of ourselves as just a few more cogs in the world's largest well-oiled machine . . . corporate America. And to be clear, when I say "corporate America," I don't mean just business behemoths. Any organization made up of a lot of people acting as a single entity working toward a common goal qualifies— profit or nonprofit. My generation grew up looking to these organizations as the place to find good careers. They were places that promised big goals, lots of room to grow and learn, well-structured compensation and benefits ensuring *security*. We wanted to be a part of those organizations, and there was an unspoken expectation that rising up the ladder in those organizations was how you measured success.

That expectation was everywhere when we were kids and young adults; it was "in the air." It painted the picture of success we carried around with us, a picture we also saw every night on television—in *Mad Men, Modern Family, Sex and the City, Suits*— not to mention in just about every commercial. It's the picture of success I saw in my own father, an ideal corporate manager, and it's the picture of success that was standard in previous generations. Success was a good job in a good organization that would take care of you as long you took care of what they asked you to do.

And if you're in one right now, maybe you, too, spend Monday to Friday waiting for the end of the workweek and the freedom of the weekend.

For me back then, Saturday was just about my only saving grace. It was the one time I could be me—could feel like me. I could wear what I wanted to wear, do what I wanted to do, talk without my bullshit banker meeting voice. I could go to brunch, hammer down mimosas and a Bloody Mary, or maybe put in a sports bet here or there. Saturday night, I could be with people I cared about and who cared about me. I didn't have to put on the fake corporate tone and small-talk nonsense I did every other day of the week. What mattered—the only thing that mattered—was that for this tiny percentage of the week, I could be me.

I'm a numbers guy, so I think about percentages, and I've done the math: if Saturday was the one and only thing I always looked forward to because it was the one and only day I felt like me, that means that I was doing the actual living of life during a twenty-four-hour period that made up only 14.3 percent of the entire week. As I write this, the average life expectancy in the US is 78.9 years, so if I'm living just 14.3 percent of every week, then out of my allotted 78.9 years, I'm actually living *my* life for only 11.3 years.

That's a bad, bad equation.

Yet this "life" was what I had been aiming for since I was nineteen and declared myself a business major in college. It's wild now to think how a "decision" I made when I was a clueless nineteen-year-old locked in the core expectation for the rest of my life. But what I really could not deal with was how, to other people anyway, the life I was leading qualified by every known definition as success.

If this was success, why the hell did I feel like there was a lid on my life pushing me down? And how far down could I go?

A New Set of Coping Mechanisms

When I arrived home on the day of my anxiety attack, I didn't have much to say to my two roommates; I desperately wanted to protect the illusion of the coolly competent rising star I was supposed to be—even from my friends. All I could think about was that what had happened to me was a sign of weakness, and that if it were revealed, it could end my career. I thought it highly unlikely that passing out in the bathroom of a prospect would "check the box" for making it into the Hi-Po group. Unable to fall asleep, I tossed and turned for hours. At around 4:00 a.m., still awake, I remembered that my health insurance plan offered a twenty-four-hour nurse hotline. I grabbed my phone and sneaked out to my car parked in the street (we had no driveway parking at the time, and I didn't want my roommates to hear me). Behind locked car doors and windows, I made the call.

"I don't know what happened to me today," I began. And then I just kept going. The nurse was a pro. She asked if I had had any suicidal thoughts. I laughed, embarrassed by the question, but she pressed on. "Situational anxiety" was her diagnosis. She didn't baby me, and she told me to see a doctor.

And I did just that. I went to see a psychiatrist because I knew that as MDs, they can prescribe drugs. What I was looking for was a way to hide the anxiety should another panic attack come on. I just didn't think my career trajectory could afford that kind of setback. First, I took Xanax, the well-known favorite for treating anxiety and panic disorders. Then I learned about beta-blockers, which slow down the fight-or-flight reflex and reduce blood pressure. I learned that they worked well for performance anxiety and were, in fact, widely used by performers I admired—actors, musicians, dancers. This clicked with me, and I began keeping beta-blockers and Xanax with me when I went to work each day. I also tried SSRIs (selective serotonin reuptake inhibitors, known mostly as antidepressants) but got off those after several months.

So the net profit of my crashing-onto-the-floor anxiety attack was the gift of a whole new set of mechanisms for coping with the Sunday Night Scaries, which clearly were not limited to Sunday night alone. I also acquired a whole new set of tools for camouflaging an oncoming blast of anxiety and stress, which happened on a fairly routine basis. What did I need to cover up? In my case, there was always a clear tip-off that some form of anxiety attack, small or large, was on the way: I would start to sweat. Hey! Perspiration is the body's cooling mechanism. But if you sweat in the middle of a perfectly regulated air-conditioning system in an office building in way upstate New York, it's not the outside temperature that's causing it; it's something else altogether. My new set of tools could prevent or at least disguise the fact that I was sweating, and that could maybe nip in the bud the anxiety attack that might follow.

That's why I was always on the lookout for clear deodorant, and it's why I kept a good supply of it at the ready. I swabbed it on my hands in case of sweaty palms, and I strategically dabbed it on my forehead and on my face so that any sweat that did occur wouldn't show. I made sure I could reach into my pockets for tissues and microdoses of Xanax or the beta-blocker propranolol—cleverly concealed, at first, in those little metal cases of Altoids. I soon realized that the cases produced a rattling sound, so I instead stuck the pills onto a strip of Listerine Cool Mint. Pretty clever, eh? I thought so, although in retrospect, it's more sad than clever, no? I figured people were assuming I was knocking back a breath sweetener, while in reality I was reaching for something to prevent the fear I kept under wraps from suddenly breaking loose.

It was thanks to all of these coping mechanisms and stop-the-sweat tools that I still went to work every day, still adapted, still muddled through, forcing myself year after year after year to fit into the role the system created for me—hot shot-on-the-rise, hitting every button on the success chart. Of course, I still fought the Sunday Night Scaries because the cause of the Scaries hadn't gone anywhere. In fact, in ten years of Sunday Night Scaries, I never even managed to ask myself what I was scared *of.* Why would I? My career was going gangbusters, I was making money, I was getting the titles and the promotions and the prestige of it all, and in my own way and with the help of Xanax and deodorant, I was coping. It never even dawned on me that there was anything odd about adjusting my behavior in this way, nor did it ever occur to me to ask myself whether I just might be selling my soul. This was the career I had planned; it was going along just fine; and I had my coping mechanisms. Rock the boat? What for?

Confrontation Time

Does any of my story sound familiar to you? Anything ring a bell? Maybe the bell is telling you that my story is an extreme, bizarre, fucked-up version of yours, but you've got to admit that you've thought about making a change to a new job, or a new industry, or a new career, or a new life.

What did you relate to in what I've just told you? My anxious Mondays maybe, or spending five days out of every seven working like hell to be true to an identity that isn't really you—a little like finding yourself onstage in a costume that looks great but is totally uncomfortable while you recite the lines from somebody else's script.

Or maybe "working from home" through the whole long pandemic just got you questioning whether you were really going to spend your whole life on a career path that suddenly looked so "safe" you might as well sleep through it.

Maybe the word *restart* in the book title ignited something inside you: It sounds so rational. It sounds like something you can do.

And you can. You can write your own script, and you can dress comfortably in your own skin as you do it. Finding a healthy, fulfilling career means doing it your way. Corporate America's thousands of for-profit and nonprofit organizations constitute one of the great engines of our economy and of our democracy; these organizations are essential players in all our lives. And within them, the possibilities for you to find the career and the lifestyle right for you are endless.

But getting to that career and lifestyle is a process. And the process is what this book is about.

I grant you that my personal restart was bizarre, to put it mildly, and you'll learn more about that in the chapters that follow. But basically, I threw it all over for a reality TV dating show, then moved back into the corporate world, then threw myself into full-time entrepreneurship because I was forced out of the bank I had begged to be forced out of. I know: it's unconventional at best, utterly wacky at worst. What I am here to tell you—what this book will show you, chapter by chapter—is the set of strategies that enabled me to put all my chips on a new opportunity without looking back. I did it because I knew that, one way or another, it would put me on a path that did not leave my life behind. What's more, I knew that if this restart came apart at the seams, I still had the strategies to continue to refresh my career. These are the very strategies I'm going to share with you.

The Eight Sharp Strategies of Restart

Throughout the remaining pages of this book, we will address these eight sharp strategies—each in its own distinct chapter—and we start with what may be the hardest: confront the truth of the life you're actually living. It's what I failed to do for as long as I could keep my reality in the closet, and if it's where you are right now, trust me, you're going to have to go back in time, do a reverse, and retrace how you got here. It's time to challenge the blueprint we all grew up with, the one that sketched out what our future should look like.

Then I'll help you create a whiteboard where you analyze what's wrong with your present career, set new priorities for the career you want, and review the practical options for achieving the career and lifestyle you seek.

Once you know where you're going, I will show you how to hack the hiring process and get or create the job you really want; how and why you always need to keep selling yourself; how networking, everybody's least favorite topic, can make all the difference in getting you to your career goals; and how to cut through the nonsense of talking about money to gain the compensation package you know you are worth.

I'll also offer what I hope are some inspirational examples of what a restart can mean to your life and happiness—as it certainly did to mine.

I can't emphasize enough, however, the importance of being totally honest as you approach each of these strategies, especially the very first, breaking the blueprint and taking a good, hard, accurate look at your life right now. It may require figuring out what you're afraid of, or delving deep into your subconscious, or articulating exactly why you're reading this book. You're going to have to overcome all that corporate training and open yourself up so you can see inside.

I used pills and clear deodorant to get through ten years of a career that was considered "super successful" by everybody but me. Believe me when I tell you that there isn't enough Xanax *or* deodorant on earth or in the heavens to keep the walls from falling in on you, especially if, like me, you put some of those walls up on your own. The chapters that follow are a whiteboard you will write on and erase and write on and erase until you identify precisely what in the past has made you unhappy, figure out precisely what you need to make you happy, and plot exactly the strategies to transition out of unhappy to happy. The only requirement is honesty.

Ready?

CHAPTER 1 RESTART REVIEW

All the Shit That's Fit to Stick

🗲 If Saturday is the one and only thing you look forward to, think about this: the average life expectancy in the US is 78.9 years, so if you're living for 14.3 percent of every week, you should expect to enjoy only 11.3 years of your life!

↻ Growing up, I always assumed that success was a good job in a good organization that would take care of me as long I did what was asked of me. One thing I didn't count on was the Sunday Night Scaries and a deep sense of unhappiness.

↻ Finding a healthy, fulfilling career means doing it your way. But getting to that career and lifestyle is a process.

↻ The first strategy may be the hardest: confront the truth of the life you're actually living. Challenge the blueprint!

↻ Identify what in the past made you unhappy, figure out what you need to make you happy, and plot exactly the strategies to transition from unhappy to happy. The only requirement is honesty.

2

Break That Damn Blueprint and Embrace Change

*B*lueprints. We all grew up with one. A blueprint was the unwritten plan for what kind of life we would live later on. It contained all those unspoken expectations and norms and pressures that we accepted without even thinking about them. They were built in, part of the structure of our lives and our families, like Thanksgiving and summer vacations. Nobody preached the blueprint to you; nobody had to. You just absorbed it: a set of behaviors to follow and actions to take to increase the likelihood of a "successful" life, according to someone or other's definition of success. Put another way, the blueprint instilled in us what we should do to personify the model of professional "accomplishment."

Who designed the blueprint and built the model? History, tradition, social customs, media, world events, our families, teachers, neighbors, friends, the time and place we find ourselves in. All of those things handed the blueprint down generation after generation to us. And everyone reading this book knows just what the blueprint for their time looked like.

At its core is the principle that a person is defined by their career. Doctor, lawyer, banker, accountant, nurse, teacher, assistant. What you do for a living is how this damn world stacks your identity. The blueprint tells us that succeeding in that career will bring us fulfillment and happiness, and it therefore stands to reason that the higher we succeed in that career, the more fulfillment and happiness we will accrue.

The blueprint also pretty much tells us what steps we should take to prepare ourselves so we can fulfill the model and gain our success. We must do well in both the classroom and in extracurricular activities while in school, kick it up a notch in high school so we can get into college, study well enough in college to pass all our courses, get a high enough GPA to be "Summa-Something," make connections, build a résumé, show degree completion, and then double-click SEND on the application to the nearest higher education admissions office, job recruiter, resource center, LinkedIn, or hell—even a job fair and get an offer for a solid, pretty-well-paying entry-level job in our selected field—most likely, the field we selected at the age of nineteen when we "declared" a major. Job offer in hand, we are on our way.

One of the things we may be on our way to is the need to pay down the student debt we incurred. As I write this, the total student debt outstanding in the US comes to $1.7 trillion and still rising,[1] which may help explain why so many people of my generation feel "locked in" to a particular job. For these debtors, a pattern of paying something but not enough to cover the full obligation means that their virtual debt load will always be a burden, locking many of them into positions they may hate just because of the importance of that biweekly deposit from their employer to cover that massive debt obligation. It means that their average debt load is increasing virtually all the time.

That is certainly what has happened with my generation of millennials. Not only that, but in general, millennials have less wealth than their parents did at the same age. They feel too financially strapped to embark on such milestones as starting a family or buying a house. I remind you: millennials are the best educated generation in US history. They—we—followed the blueprint to the letter.

Even without the burden of debt, the blueprint can sometimes feel like a trap. Whether we stop at the BA degree or go on to a profession that requires graduate study, such as medicine, law, engineering, accounting, or architecture, the fact is that once that first position is landed, it seems more comfortable and maybe easier to continue to rise in it step by predetermined step till retirement.

That's the blueprint I was following, and if it had all worked that smoothly, well, shit! I wouldn't have been passing out in bathrooms, no publisher would be interested in what I have to say, and you wouldn't be reading a book about how the hell to change course and restart your career and your life.

The truth is that the blueprint we were all born into has a couple of significant flaws. If you want to see what one of them looks like, take a look at some of the most successful people of our time. How about billionaire innovators Bill Gates and Mark Zuckerberg—college dropouts, both of them. Or Oprah Winfrey, born in poverty to a single teenage mother, who just happened to land a job in radio when she was in high school—and took it from there. Or world-renowned author Stephen King, who worked as a janitor, gas pump attendant, laundry worker, and teacher and churned out a raft of forgettable short stories to pay the rent and put food on the table till he hit it big with *Carrie*—then never looked back. Or *Shark Tank*'s beloved Shark, Barbara Corcoran, who failed at twenty-two jobs by the age of twenty-three—one for every year except infancy!—eventually losing her boyfriend to the affair he had with their secretary before he assured her that she would "never succeed without me."

The blueprint we were all born into
has a couple of significant flaws.

Of course you've heard of Etsy. Well, before Rob Kalin created that website, he managed to fail almost every course in high school except art and was a deadbeat in the eyes of his parents. Etsy now has a market cap, as of this writing, of nearly $35 billion.

And then there's Lady Gaga, who dropped out of the prestigious Tisch School of the Arts at New York University so she could keep singing at open mic nights and pursue the career she believed she was meant to have.

Blueprint breakers, all of them. Stubbornly and persistently, they listened to what they alone could hear, strayed from the blueprint to follow their own individual paths, and gained a level of success most of us can only dream about.

I know: you're not a Bill Gates or a Lady Gaga. Neither am I. They and the others are individuals driven by a kind of genius, a drive that they simply refuse to set aside. They are exceptions and unique; each of them one of a kind. Most of us can't aspire to their genius, and we probably can't achieve what they've achieved. We can't emulate their success, but we *can* emulate what ultimately made them so successful: their willingness to break the blueprint written for them and follow the journey they saw ahead of them.

There's another important incentive that may help convince you to detour from the traditional blueprint: that blueprint isn't actually working very well anymore. There are a shit ton of red flags indicating that the model of success it promises might not be accomplishing what it claims to.

Two Sides to Every Story

Remember the college admissions scandal that erupted in 2019 and that caught a bunch of wealthy parents, including Hollywood celebs, in a conspiracy to get their kids into prestigious colleges? Parents paid an outfit called Edge College & Career Network LLC either to take entrance tests for their kids or to bribe college athletic coaches to "recruit" the kids as athletes, whether they could play the sport at all or not. While some celebs—notably Felicity Huffman and Lori Loughlin—got prison sentences as a result, Rick Singer, who founded the Edge Network, as of this writing has yet to serve a day. The scandal was the subject of a fine documentary, *Operation Varsity Blues*.

For me, the scandal highlighted something that I found both ugly and sad as well as kind of shocking: the lengths some people would go to put themselves and their kids at the very epicenter of the blueprint. Whether it really was for the benefit of their children or to satisfy their own egos, these parents committed fraud to game the blueprint—the all-important, do-whatever-you-can-to-succeed-at-it blueprint. They risked and lost their good names, and they caused enormous harm to the very people they thought they were helping: their children.

Sure, we all know that some very rich people will donate serious bucks to elite schools to get their kids "acceptance" through a kind of side door. It stings for those who would never get that shortcut, and it sucks for those whose spot they are taking. We also all went to high school with people who claimed they knew they "had to take every AP class" the school offered—whatever the cost in sleep, fun, health—so as to get into a school their parents would approve of. If parents think they are doing their kids a favor by beating the drum for this kind of prestige, they are dead wrong.

So it's time to ask if the blueprint isn't at least one reason that depression is the leading cause of disability in the US among people fifteen to thirty-five and why it ranks among the top three health disasters in the workplace, where it is estimated to cost some $210.5 billion per year in lost earnings.[2] In the years 2009 to 2012 alone, according to the Centers for Disease Control and Prevention's National Health survey, 5.8 percent of people in the eighteen to thirty-nine age group and 7.2 percent in the forty to fifty-nine age group reported feeling depressed, dejected, and despondent—along with the typical side effects of lack of energy and loss of sleep.

Also, suicide is the second leading cause of death for people aged fifteen to forty-four.

Doesn't this at the least tell us that many changes are necessary?

Yes, divorce is down. The Centers for Disease Control and Prevention tells us that the average divorce rate in the US in 2019 showed a 32.5 percent decrease from the year 2000.[3] That sounds like good news, right? Not really. In fact, the decrease is attributed as much to couples' financial inability to pay for divorce as to the strength of conjugal ties. Also, the rate of total marriages is down, meaning that people are marrying later in life.[4] This suggests that those people at least may be pulling away from the traditional blueprint, deciding to gain a bit more maturity and perhaps more economic stability before committing to marriage.

For those at work, meanwhile, the statistics remain bleak. A comprehensive study on job satisfaction, conducted jointly by the Lumina Foundation, the Bill & Melinda Gates Foundation, Omidyar Network, and Gallup, and reported on in *Forbes*, found that *less than half* of workers described their jobs as good. Forty-one percent of the thirty thousand people polled—from a variety of companies across thirty-one countries—said they were "mulling" leaving their jobs.[5] Fifty-four percent said they were overworked; 39 percent were exhausted. Maybe it is worth asking if such statistics are another side product of following the blueprint.

At the Nexus

Tell me about it. When I began my banking career, my definition of success was totally based in the traditional blueprint instilled in me from day one of my life. Success to me was about chasing money, responsibility, power, and titles. Hey, let's be real: you meet someone and within two minutes, you're asking each other, "What do you do?" It's like this weird strategy to immediately stack someone up—as if their fucking title tells you who they are as a person or signals their actual wealth. But there I was chasing the title, so that in the twenty-second convo that follows "Whatdoyoudo," I could sound like I had something going for me and could meet or exceed the subconscious expectation of success I could see in the other person's eyes. I chased titles because the next higher title meant the next step up to impress people in the next "Whatdoyoudo" convo—a higher step on both the money front and the respect front. The money part is easy to calculate, but believe me, the respect front can be pretty gratifying too— even if, as I would soon learn, it is empty. It is gratifying because it is just a better means of feeding the ego: that is, better a senior banker than a junior banker, and not just in front of your subordinates and peers. You also get a bit more attentiveness from your family, friends, and—shit! as weird as this sounds—even from your bartender. When bartenders hear "senior banker," they figure your corporate card limit just shot up. So, for me, achievement meant success all day long, but that was driven by ego. For most of us, after all, ego is in the driver's seat, and until we proactively self-correct, ego rather than utility becomes the driving force.

When nobody was looking, I knew how unhappy I was and how empty my life felt.

It was only when I got home from work that the bottom fell out of all that self-satisfaction. When nobody was looking, I knew how unhappy I was and how empty my life felt.

It all began to remind me of a story told to me by my mother's father, my grandpa Lenny. The story was about what happened when, as a young man, he announced to his father, my great-grandfather Dave, that he wanted to be a singer and to perform live onstage. Great-Grandpa Dave replied simply, "That's not going to happen." He told his son that "in this family, what you are going to do is become a professional—a doctor, a lawyer, or an accountant. Period."

Grandpa Lenny complied, became a successful endodontist and an esteemed professor, a pillar of his community, beloved and respected, sharing with his cousins the honor of the family's last name on a gymnasium building on the campus of the University of Buffalo—a life that was a credit to his family and himself. But he also told me that he always regretted not having taken a shot at his dream.

My grandfather lived in a different time, to be sure. His father's family had been immigrants, part of that wave of European Jews who back then came to this country to escape persecution; they came here for safety—simply to survive. I'm sure Great-Grandpa Dave was grateful to have found that safety, and I think what he was telling his son was to opt for "security" and acceptance and not to do anything that might rock the boat.

Alone in my apartment at the end of the day, when my latest brighter-than-ever corporate title wasn't much compensation for the emptiness I felt in my life, I thought about Grandpa Lenny sometimes. Yes, I was moving up fast. I was getting killer performance reviews: "Jason has a unique perspective on client service. . . ." "Jason successfully hit and quickly exceeded the goals set. . . ." "This opportunity arose *because* we had Jason as a resource. . . ." Not to mention one promotion after another.

Some of the promotions were also relocations; one even took me to corporate headquarters right at the center of the action.

Working at corporate HQ was like being in the middle of what I imagine a king's court was like back in medieval times. It was also a lot like high school with cliques of Hi-Po guys and girls. Everybody there was hell-bent not just on getting close to the those with power and clout—the top rung of executives, who were the royalty of HQ—but of being *seen to be close*. It was a game played out with deadly seriousness at the Starbucks right next to the elevator leading up to the executive suite. Booking a coffee with a key exec—and being seen with that exec at a table in front of Starbucks before "office hours"—was the ultimate token of success. It meant you were "in" with the power crowd, on your way to being knighted by the king. I fell for it, participated in it, but I do remember thinking that it was some real nauseating bullshit. I should have listened more closely to that voice in my head.

I didn't. I kept relocating. And guess what: my sense of emptiness relocated with me wherever I went. I began to wonder if it wasn't time to do what Grandpa Lenny said he always regretted *not* doing: to follow my dream. The problem was that this *was* my dream. Rising up the ladder in corporate America was exactly what I had been striving for. I had relied on a hand-me-down definition of career success—the blueprint—without ever turning inward to ask myself what I really wanted to do in my life, without ever thinking about what kind of life would be in tune with who I am and what makes me happy.

That's precisely what I'm asking you to do, however, and I'm suggesting that you do it right now.

Breaking the Blueprint

When I arrived in the bank's Seattle office ready to take on the job I had been aiming for since my first day at work, it was not my first visit. Dispatched there by the "royalty" at the company as the man for the job, I was interviewed up and down the Seattle hierarchy in several cross-country visits. Me. In person. Long slicked-back hair, clean shaven, in my boring banker's black suit with white shirt and red tie. That's how I showed up; that's how they hired me—they, the hierarchy in Seattle.

And then, in a stunningly passive-aggressive move, they told me I had to change my physical appearance. Specifically, my hair. It wasn't "right," I was told, for my title or for "the way we do things in Seattle." Cut it, they told me, much shorter, and ease up on all the gel. I actually felt terrible for my boss because I could see in his eyes that it actually pained him to make this request. I got the feeling that he found it ridiculous and didn't like having to play bad cop at the request of the regional president. But that's how this world works. Do as you are told by the "royals," and do it with a smile on your face if you want to get by. Smiles can easily lie; eyes rarely can.

It was almost my breaking point. Clearly, this should have told me that you can't keep following the blueprint forever. Even when it varies from company to company, leadership to leadership, state to state, and city to city. It's still there! Eventually, you fail at it—presumably when you hit the point where you just can't live someone else's life anymore. Instead of doing that, I just felt like a coward and continued to play the game, telling myself it didn't matter so much; it was just hair. What saved me was friends from back home in Rochester who dubbed the incident "Seattle Hairgate" and made a joke out of it. Only by laughing at it could I live with it. But not for much longer. I just didn't know how to break the blueprint.

Now I do.

How Did Your Blueprint Get Built?

Think back to when you were growing up. What were the expectations you heard around the dinner table? Did your parents influence your thoughts on what you should "be" or do when you grew up? Did they help "direct" your education toward a specific career? What about friends? Teachers? Coaches? Did they make suggestions, offer opinions, turn you away from some of your thinking, or turn you toward another way of thinking? Are you in the career you're in because of what you decided to major in in college when you were eighteen? Or because you are replicating the path you saw a family member or friend follow? What were the small influences that brought you step by step to where you are now, what you do, and why you feel stuck?

Maybe you never needed to hear from or be influenced by others. Maybe, like me, you just always "knew." I think for me I always "knew" because I never found a reason to think outside what seemed obvious. As I mentioned, going into a business in corporate America was pretty standard for the time and place in which I grew up. I really wasn't terribly aware of other options, and I certainly wasn't sure how to pursue anything else. I think most of this comes with time, but if you could solve this hack and zoom out earlier, the awareness of options that it brings can become a massive superpower.

Restart Right Now?

DO YOU NEED a restart? Ask yourself these questions:

- ⚡ Would you continue on with this job if you were paid half of what you're making?
- ⚡ Do you feel you are on the right path—the dream path—to where you want to arrive?
- ⚡ Do you wake up in the mornings excited to get to the next meeting, the next planning session, the next performance review?
- ⚡ Is your work creating the legacy you've always wanted to leave?

> ⚡ Are you positioned to be out of debt in the coming years?
>
> ⚡ Can you imagine being with the same company in five, ten, fifteen years from now?
>
> ⚡ If you were on your deathbed looking back, would this career, title, and position make you feel incredibly proud?
>
> ⚡ Are you living the life you always imagined?
>
> ⚡ Are you maximizing the greatest impact that your skill set, acumen, and abilities offer?
>
> If you have answered no to any of these questions, then you don't have a week, a day, or even an hour to wait. You need to be open to restarting right here, right now. That means embracing the idea that you will break the blueprint you have been following and will catapult yourself out of the day-to-day autopilot that has become a habit.

Did you ever know anybody who *did* break the blueprint? I'm thinking of the kid in my neighborhood who knew from the time he was little that he wanted to grow up to be a part of Broadway theater—the Great White Way—even though he sometimes got bullied or picked on by other kids for expressing that dream, which looked so out of sync with the blueprint that had the rest of us hooked. The kid I'm talking about was always tops academically but maybe an outcast to the "cool" kids. He was the kid who challenged the system and carried the dream with him right to the real thing, leaving the small town to go to the big city for college, then from college to a job right where he wanted to be, and then from the job to becoming owner of a company that does the marketing for virtually every well-known Broadway show.

Maybe you had a friend or an acquaintance like that, and maybe you questioned what they were doing and wondered how they could be so sure about something that seemed so "off the charts" to everyone else. For me, that "kid" was my brother. I watched him step by step, year by year, as he went on to lead the life he always dreamed of. From a distance, I saw his successes and failures, gains and losses—student council leadership among the highs, bullies making fun of him among the indignities. But I was there when he landed the high school lead as Prince Charming in *Cinderella*, and I was there when he escorted us backstage at *Hamilton, the* hottest ticket on Broadway, where he introduced us to the cast, clearly friends and admirers of my big brother. I saw it right in front of my face and almost still couldn't believe it, but I sure did feel proud to be his bro.

People like my brother are the exceptions, I think. And I envy them for finding their dream early and for pursuing it. But I think the truth is that the rest of us have just sleepwalked our way into careers that no longer bring us satisfaction—if they ever did.

That's why it's time to wake up, analyze and define the blueprint that got you where you are today, break it, and think anew—with a definition of success that you alone create.

What is your definition of success for you, on your terms?

If, like me, you always looked at success in terms of the title, the financial package, the promotions, you already know that's not enough. It's time instead to look at success in terms of what it means to you personally—that is, how you want to live your life. In my case, I never laid my cards out on the table about what I wanted my life to be. The result? I was successful within the confines of the office; when I got home at night, my life was a disaster. I was alone, I had not particularly enjoyed the day at the office, and I was not especially proud of the work I did. How does this add up to success?

The question is simple: What is your definition of success for you, on your terms? The time to answer it is now, with this warning: do not present your answer in silos. I'm not asking for a definition of professional success and another for personal success. I'm asking for one answer that correlates the two. That's what is essential in order to restart your career. And, of course, nobody can answer the question for you.

Once you have answered the question, it changes everything. The answer becomes your tool for snapping out of the near hypnosis in which the blueprint has held you. You're back in charge of yourself, no longer swayed by the suggestions or advice of others. Once you have broken the blueprint, you'll be in a position to correlate your definition of success as your life mission—your main source of energy for prescribing what comes next in terms of job, career, and lifestyle. The next step is to align that definition to the external strategy we're about to build, the strategy that will get you to your restart.

But to make it work, you're going to have to get vulnerable.

CHAPTER 2 RESTART REVIEW

All the Shit That's Fit to Stick

- ⟡ Most of us can't aspire to a Bill Gates or Lady Gaga level of genius, and we probably can't achieve what they've achieved. But we can emulate what made them successful.

- ⟡ Blueprint breakers, all of them. Stubbornly and persistently, they listened to what they alone could hear, strayed from the blueprint to follow their own individual paths, and gained a level of success most of us can only dream about.

- ⟡ A comprehensive study on job satisfaction found that fewer than half of workers described their jobs as good.

- ⟡ But I think the truth is that the rest of us have just sleepwalked our way into careers that no longer bring us satisfaction—if they ever did. That's why it's time to wake up, analyze and define the blueprint that got you where you are today, break it, and think anew—with a definition of success that you alone create.

❧ If you always looked at success in terms of title, pay, and promotions, you already know that's not enough. It's time instead to look at success in terms of what it means to you personally and how you want to live your life.

❧ What is your definition of success for you, on your terms? Once you have answered the question, it changes everything.

3

The Efficacy of Vulnerability

*R*emember the story that opened this book—my scary panic attack on the floor of the men's room? The truth is I had never actually revealed that incident to a living soul—not to a friend, a significant other, a family member, no one—until I spilled it all in this book. Am I embarrassed thinking about it, talking about it, and reliving it? I sure am. In fact, dealing with embarrassment had long been an issue for me. I always wanted to be seen as strong, smart, and composed—not weak or panic-driven to the point of passing out on a bathroom floor. But if I am asking you to be vulnerable with yourself, I sure ought to be vulnerable with you. So yes, I am open to thousands of readers and former coworkers and bosses learning that a guy they may have thought of as always optimistic, full of positive energy, a composed character on a reality TV show is actually a guy who fled a high-level corporate meeting and was reduced to a pathetic bundle of panic on the floor of the nearest executives-only freaking toilet. Only to then hide Xanax and beta-blockers in a Listerine strip case to prevent history from repeating itself.

But that is the level of vulnerability and honesty you are going to need to make this exercise in self-examination effective. And I figure if I am asking for that level of vulnerability and honesty from you, you deserve the same from me. The path to restart begins precisely there.

To understand why, think construction. You're ready to move out of or tear down the career you're in and to build something different. When building or rebuilding any structure, you need to start with the foundation; if it is flawed, the new structure simply won't stand. Same thing in building a new way to make a living: you need to go deep into self-examination, right down to the bedrock of what isn't working for you, of what simply does not feel true to who you are.

This is not an exercise in surface-level complaints such as an unfair boss or an inadequate salary. Those complaints are too easy. You could probably sit down right now and come up with any number of things about your job that you would like to change. Maybe it's work-life balance. Maybe it's a feeling of uncertainty about whether you're good at it. Maybe it's your equivalent of my Sunday Night Scaries. Or the hunger for a richer benefits package. The company culture. Your coworkers. Your title. Misgivings about the product you work to sell. Insecurity about how you come off to others. Where you live. Subtle embarrassment when you tell people the name of your company or what you do for a living. It isn't difficult to come up with all sorts of things about a job or career that you would like to change.

But to really get it done, you're going to have to go deeper than that, and you're going to have to get raw about what isn't working for you. That's what I mean by vulnerability, and I can assure you that the change you're looking for just won't happen without it.

Ditto for honesty. Again, the honesty I'm talking about has little to do with the sort of low-level, who-could-it-hurt fabrications we all indulge in. Think instead about your annual physical: when the doctor asks how many alcoholic drinks you imbibe in a week, answering "maybe a couple but only on Saturday" isn't going to help the doc help you. (Unless, of course, that's really the sum total of your alcoholic intake.) Diagnosis demands absolute honesty—no bullshit.

So think of this book as a journey for you and only you. One where you can self-reflect and think openly and widely, free from unspoken pressures or outside forces. No one is here to judge you, argue with you, or harp on you to be any other way than what your creative brain tells you. Everything is *not* perfect, and on this journey, you must embrace those imperfections because they are putting you on the path from fake smiles to proud eyes. This is for you and only you, so let's address the flat-out reality and the fears you've never faced. It's essential: I promise you here and now that digging deep enough to hit absolute truth in your self-examination is a necessity for creating the future you want. You simply cannot restructure, reroute, or make the detour you want to make without peeling down to the core of the life and the career you're in right now. To that end, I hereby grant you permission to be selfish—to put yourself first as you go through this process.

And I'm going to walk you through the process, guiding you through a methodology that will enable you to identify the precise sources of your dissatisfaction, then forge them into a path toward change.

Defining What's Not Working

For openers, I want you to consult what I'll call your "inner circle." Pick anywhere from two to five people you absolutely trust, people who know you well and who care about you. Ask them to tell you—right off the top of their head—what they think of three things: the company you work for, your title and position, and your professional career overall. No prep, no lead-in; you want their first-reaction answers. Write them down.

Then go sit alone in a room with a pad of paper or a whiteboard or a voice or video recorder—no other tech at all—and look at the sum total of the feedback you've received. Now write down the real facts of your life and career. Be as honest with yourself as I was with you: What are your "equivalents" of the panic attacks, or the Xanax, or the feeling of being in handcuffs five days out of seven? No one is there to hear you or see you; no one is looking over your shoulder. This is your chance to tell yourself the real truth of your career. It is your Career Dissatisfaction Checklist—an inventory of what to discard and avoid in the career you really want.

INNER CIRCLE SAYS . . .	MY FACTS

My inner circle for this exercise comprised my mother and father, my girlfriend at the time, and one of my closest buddies. I found the words they came up with pretty interesting. *Secure. Successful. Stable. Go-getter. Impressive title. Promotable. Great money. Going places.* They were words that catalogued the kind of career I had set out to have but now felt alien from. The Career Dissatisfaction Checklist that I then scribbled on a piece of paper was the kickoff for my restart. The truth you write down in your checklist will be the starting point for yours as well.

Career Dissatisfaction: A Self-Examination Through Five Career Determinants

The process I'm about to introduce to you proceeds strategically, unwinding across five core issues that I've identified as the essential determinants of any career:

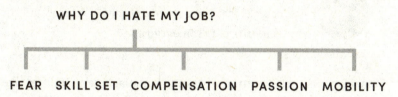

WHY DO I HATE MY JOB?

FEAR   SKILL SET   COMPENSATION   PASSION   MOBILITY

Why these five? For one thing, everything you've written down or voice-recorded in your Dissatisfaction Checklist fits into one or more of those five buckets. Guaranteed. In addition, my own experience, my consulting work, the many talks I've given, and the feedback I've taken in confirm for me that these five are the forces that decide the nature of a career. They're the pillars of a career, the things that give it its essential character. So identifying where you locate yourself on each and how each shapes what's critical to you provides the big reveal: the map that will lead the way to change.

For example, suppose I ask you to imagine yourself ten years from now at the same company you work for today but making four times the money you're making now and with the title of executive vice president. If your reaction is "Wow! That would make me happy," it suggests that the issues that define a good career for you are Compensation and Mobility: what you make and how high you rise. That's a directional signal. It's pointing you to what has to change—a particular amount of money and a particular place in the hierarchy—for you to be happy in your career.

Just as I promised: vulnerability is amazingly efficient.

So find a fresh piece of paper or a clean whiteboard or put your phone on silent and use the Notes app on your iPhone and proceed slowly as you examine yourself one career determinant at a time. Remember: get vulnerable and be scrupulously honest.

SKILL SET

 Jason Tartick @Jason_Tartick
Are the skills that make you *you* aligned to your job, to your company, or to something else?

Do you ever sit in a meeting with senior management and feel like the imposter in the room? Worse, do you sit in a meeting with your *peers* and feel like an imposter? You may be all too familiar with "imposter syndrome," that awful feeling that you don't belong, that you lack the talent, the status, the skills, the wherewithal to do the job while everybody around you has it all. It's often fused with cultural and class issues as well. Maybe you didn't do well enough in school, or you went to the "wrong" school, or perhaps you just don't have the same résumé or experiences. None of this defines you, of course, but such worries can be hard to fight.

I had to fight it big-time on the first night of *The Bachelorette* when I got out of the limo and walked into the mansion to meet my fellow suitors for Becca Kufrin. Oh boy! What do I see but about thirty absolute studs: tall, jacked, beautiful-looking, sharply dressed dudes. Then we began chatting and oh boy! again. Some of these guys were major-league ballplayers, some were in the NFL, another was a Harlem Globetrotter. Even one of the founders of Venmo was there. Others talked about their huge jobs, managed to let me know their huge titles, and reported on their huge

achievements. One guy told me within seconds of being introduced that he had been featured on four magazine covers. (For
my Bachelor Nation fans: that was, of course, Jordan Kimball!)

And I thought to myself: I'm an average dude from Buffalo, New
York, and I'm a banker. In my little world, playing Division III soc-
cer was solid; in here it was like, "joke show." So how do I compete
with this? These guys are all taller, bigger, faster, stronger, and with
cooler jobs than me. How did I get put in the same room with
them? And, oh shit, we're all competing for the same woman?
Lovely.

I had the feeling that I just didn't belong. Classic imposter
syndrome.

The truth is, however, if you were invited to the mansion or
have a seat at the conference room table, there's a reason for it.
Which means you *do* belong there. Otherwise, I guess I wouldn't
have been one of thirty accepted out of hundreds of thousands
that apply. The only question you need to ask is whether your
skill set—the range of your natural talents and learned abilities—
aligns with the position you hold and the company you work for,
and whether and how to magnify that skill set alignment to advance your career. That's the issue. It's not the composition of
your skill set or the number of skills. It's whether your skills
align with the work you have been tasked to do and with the
company's purpose.

That first night of *The Bachelorette*, the more I talked with
these impressive studs and suitors, the more I realized that a lot
of them had plenty of ego but not very much self-awareness. They
seemed more worried about themselves and the vibes they were
giving off than about the reason we were all there—to date Becca.
They were definitely taller, bigger, with more impressive stories
of success. There was no way I could match all that. I had never
been an NFL linebacker, did not run my own hedge fund or create
a wildly popular e-commerce website, and could not do a backflip

while dunking a basketball. But then I realized that being from Buffalo and shorter than the other guys wasn't the issue. This "contest" wasn't about height or title. It was about knowing what differentiates me. And where that was concerned, I had some strengths of my own. I could read and react to a situation, be aware of all the moving parts from producers to suitors, and communicate effectively with all of these guys without needing to attract attention to who I was.

Once I knew my own value, my own differentiating strength, I felt comfortable in my ability to be effective on the show and to have fun doing it. Stay under the radar, befriend them all, do not pose a threat, speak less, listen more, and use all the information gathered to my advantage. Worked like a charm. And before I knew it, it was the egos and emotional imbalance of the majority that led to their "demise."

After *The Bachelorette*, I was on *Celebrity Family Feud*, hosted by Steve Harvey. Speaking of imposter syndrome, we played against the Victoria's Secret Angels! Anyway, Steve liked to chat with the audience during commercials, and in one of these chats, a woman in the audience said to him, "Hey, hosting looks cool! How can I get a hosting job like you?"

"This idea of wanting to do what seems cool is interesting," said Steve. He paused. "You know what I think would be cool?" he went on. "I think it would be cool to be a pro golfer. But that's not going to happen. Wanna know why? I love golf so much I'd love to play it every day, and you know what? I *suck* at golf! I just can't play golf well at all." Instead, Steve told the woman, you have to dig deep inside, test your skills, find out what you're good at, and differentiate yourself at that. "Here's what I'm good at," Steve said. "I'm good at being in front of a crowd and talking as honestly as possible to someone I've never met before." He went on: "But if I tried to make a living at golf, I'd still be living out of my car in Cleveland because I absolutely suck at golf!"

Finding my differentiated skill set is what defined my career at the bank, where, as in most banks, there are two main types of skill sets: the relationship building/business development/interpersonal networking skill sets that obtained and cared for clients, and the mastery of all things analytical that kept the business of banking working for the clients. I excelled at the former. I outperformed not just the analytical sharks, who weren't really expected to be good at interpersonal networking, but also many of my smarter and better educated fellow "relationship builders." When I broke it down, it was clear that while I wasn't as analytical as the analytical sharks, I knew the places where I could outperform them. And while I also wasn't as good at the business development and the relationship building as the geniuses at the top of the tree, I knew I had sharper analytical skills than they did. That particular combination was my differentiating skill set. It was uniquely *me*, and it aligned to my relationship-banking career. It is unquestionably why I accelerated at such a fast pace. The problem was that within the bank at the time, there simply wasn't the opportunity to grow that unique skill set as high and wide as I was ready to. There was a ceiling on how high and how well I could continue to exploit my differentiating strengths. The result was that I simply kept moving around *inside* the organization, holding seven different jobs over the period of ten years—and the impact on me became pretty stultifying.

So take Steve Harvey's words to heart when you begin your "assignment" to see where you are in terms of skill set. Define *exactly* what makes you uniquely you—the precise skill set that differentiates you from your peers and that comes as naturally to you as hosting does to Steve Harvey. Give yourself the answer right now, while the question is fresh in your mind: What package of talents and abilities and strengths of character and traits of personality set you apart from everyone around you? Write it down. Copy and paste it onto your mind. For that is the skill set you want to nourish and develop in order to propel your career forward and upward. You don't need anyone else helping you to identify this skill set: neither your boss, nor your boss's boss, nor your colleagues know what sets you apart, and you certainly don't want other people's values defining you. Identify carefully and truthfully the unique skill set that makes you *you*, and you'll never feel like an imposter. Then decide if and how you can align that skill set to your current job, your current company, or another situation where it can grow your career.

COMPENSATION

Jason Tartick @Jason_Tartick
Be honest and real . . . do you think you're paid fairly for the work you do?

While it feels like compensation ought to be an absolutely straightforward measure of career satisfaction, in fact it's anything *but*. Yes, the questions you need to ask are pretty unambiguous: Are you being compensated appropriately for the value you add? Do the bonuses or raises you get correlate to the work you do and the value you bring to it? Are your performance reviews rating you fairly, appropriately, and according to a clear and pertinent set of measurements?

When I started out, compensation was my number one issue and my top priority, and as soon as I decided that the compensation I was getting was way off what it ought to be, I took action: I left. I took another job, one in a different industry—selling data services—that also brought me closer to home. Nine months later, I arranged to meet with a senior banker from the corporate banking group of my former employer, hoping she might give some referrals for people at the branch to whom I could make my sales pitch. We talked about data services and about banking, and the meeting suddenly changed into her pitching me to come back to the bank. Her pitch won, and I ended up pursuing an interview to go back to the bank. When they made the actual job offer, I demanded a whole different compensation package—and got it: a more-than-50-percent raise over my previous salary there—all by leaving nine months earlier and coming back!

A few years later, I again thought my compensation was not what it ought to be; it did not seem to me to match outside marketplace expectations. I wasn't thinking about the marketplace expectations for my age group or for people with similar educational credentials. Rather, I wanted to find out whether I was being compensated in accordance with marketplace expectations for what *I* brought to the table and for *my* performance.

My strategy was to go right to a group of recruiters looking for bankers in the area. I reached out, told them who I was and where I worked, recited my performance reviews for the year, and asked each for a verbal offer of what compensation I could expect. I took those offers to my then boss and made my case: "I don't want to leave, but I have been offered a base salary 31.5 percent higher than I am now getting." Within forty-eight hours, I was given a 20 percent raise to stay where I was. And I did.

My point was made: for me, compensation was a key determinant of career satisfaction; if it wasn't right in my eyes, neither was the job, and I had to act.

If compensation is a key determinant for you, then you want to be able to have an impact on ensuring that it is working for you as it should. If that isn't the case in the job or career you now have, that's a message you can't afford to dismiss. There'll be much more on this subject of compensation—and how to get it—in chapter nine.

●　●　●

MOBILITY

Jason Tartick @Jason_Tartick
Where will your current career take you? Does your employer have a plan to take you to that place . . . and is that the place you want your life to be?

Imagine that you got an offer to go on *The Bachelor* or *The Bachelorette,* but you knew you'd be eliminated on night one. Would you go? Unless you're one in a million—that would be Grocery Store Joe—the answer should be no. Why?

First, it's got to be embarrassing, and second, there's no mobility!

But let's go from reality TV to actual reality again. The question is similar: Where can your current job or career path take you? To answer, you need to look clearly at the opportunities available, at your company's commitment to developing talent, and at the flexibility and expansiveness within your chosen industry. Ask yourself whether the company's commitment is expressed in reasonable goals and expectations, with systems of accountability in place and adhered to. It is not unknown for companies to set unreasonable standards for mobility, reward only the top 10 percent, and get away with it. You need to know precisely what support for your mobility you can expect from your boss and even from your coworkers.

The heart of the matter is, obviously, highly personal. Your company's commitment to mobility will affect where you go from here and will define the opportunities to rise in the job or career you now have. Logically, without stretching your imagination too far, you want to assess where you can be fifteen years from right now.

List the scenarios. Write them down.

But after probing *where* you can go, there's an equally vital question to ask: Is what you see fifteen years ahead a place you want to be? So play a head game with those future possible scenarios and place yourself in each one of the opportunities you've identified. See yourself there, fifteen years from now. What does it look like? How does it feel? And if you're saying to yourself, "Jason, fifteen years of planning is way too far out," I'll tell you about one of the most brilliant individuals I've ever interviewed, business tycoon and host of many MTV shows, Rob Dyrdek. He has a five-hundred-year plan related to the Dyrdek Family Mission—and he updates it annually!

In my case, I started out totally gung-ho for rising through the ranks as fast as possible to the top. And I acted accordingly, promising my bosses I would go anywhere and do anything, busting my chops, sacrificing personal relationships because I was spending so much time moving so fast, changing locations to seize new promotions, switching to different areas within the organization, wearing myself out—till I got exactly where I wanted to be: *the* job at the right compensation, three thousand miles from home, and at the top of my game. After ten years, this was it!

This was it? This was what I had sacrificed my energy and my time and had expended enormous effort to achieve? I could do the job by rote, it barely engaged my attention, and my new location— Seattle—left me feeling out of place and lonely. Let me tell you: the realization that where you want to be isn't at all where you want to be is pretty mind-boggling. And when I looked at where I could go from there, all of the promotions still awaiting me looked and felt utterly empty. I realized there was simply nowhere up ahead where I wanted to go. For me, at least, that's when I knew I had to make a change, and I jumped headlong into something that I figured would at least shake me up: a reality TV show. (And it did.)

But you have an opportunity to take the time I couldn't even sit still for and to think ahead. A career can last a long time, and if you want to keep yours fresh and satisfying, it's essential to think about exactly where you want it to take you and how you want to get there. Dissatisfaction with a fancier title and a bigger bonus can still be dissatisfaction. So it's essential to look hard at the direction and effectiveness of the mobility you can achieve, versus detouring into a career change. After enduring this restart process, you may realize that several tweaks can actually optimize your current situation such that a full detour may not be necessary.

FEAR

Jason Tartick @Jason_Tartick
In truth, in the corporate world, we are all free agents, and very damned few of us are a LeBron James, Tom Brady, or Serena Williams commanding multimillion-dollar long-term stratospheric salaries in return for our skills and abilities.

Let's face it: organizations thrive on complacency. They count on the assumption that you are content in your pretty good job at a pretty good salary and that, clearly, the last thing you would ever want to do is risk losing that job. Simply put, people who are afraid do not rock the boat. Organizations count on that. Your fear inspires your complacency and is the core of your loyalty to the organization and all its demands. Fear-to-complacency-to-loyalty is the fuel that keeps the organization going and you contentedly in your place. To many, it is *the* determining issue for avoiding a career change; even the thought of shifting where you are raises the fear level and strengthens the complacency.

I know that my complacency during my decade in corporate America showed up in my being overly loyal to my boss, whoever he or she was at the moment. I effectively promised each boss: "Put me wherever you want to put me, assign me whatever task you can, move me to whatever location you decide, and I'll do everything you ask." And I did. Call it loyalty to the nth degree.

But loyalty, as everybody knows, is supposed to be a two-way street, so what about the organization's loyalty to you? How does your company repay you for your willingness to be loyally complacent? It simply doesn't. In truth, in the corporate world, we are all free agents, and very damned few of us are a LeBron James, Tom Brady, or Serena Williams commanding multimillion-dollar long-term stratospheric salaries in return for our skills and abilities. In the corporate world, security in return for complacency is simply not part of the package, and there isn't a contract that can't be broken or "renegotiated." It really means that you're always a free agent who can be let loose at any time into the big, wide marketplace, looking for the next possibility. All it takes is one "mistake," one foot put wrong for one minute. Anyone can get axed.

That can be scary. It is risky. And that scary risk of the unknown quite simply frightens many of us away from the very idea of making a change. So we stay complacent until it just no longer seems possible, not if we're going to feel alive at all.

When I returned to my job at the bank after my stint on *The Bachelorette*, I had a sterling reputation, both as a banker and as a reality TV personality. In fact, management wanted to take advantage of that, to use my celebrity to represent the brand. So I was tasked to fill speaking engagements and to host benefit events for nonprofit organizations in the bank's name—a busy schedule for which I always showed up and always did my best.

Then one day on her podcast, my then-girlfriend-later-fiancé made one off-the-cuff, rather funny comment about something sexual. The next second, my free agency was in effect: I was out. Ten years of commitment to the job and the organization, consistently excellent performance reviews, four relocations to three different states, even extending my own public celebrity to the bank's advantage might just as well never have happened. Just like that, I was dropped like a deadweight for a remark someone else made on a podcast! Call it a damning example of corporate "loyalty" to the employees who are any organization's most important resource.

Any lingering doubts I may have had about cutting the cord and restarting my career and my life went out the door that same second. Ever hear the expression, "With friends like that, who needs enemies?" My sentiments exactly.

As you examine your own situation and your own relationship to the organization you work for, let my sudden "free agency" serve as a reminder to take a cold, hard look at any fears or sense of reluctance you may have about making a change.

PASSION

Jason Tartick @Jason_Tartick
The *only* thing left of my career was the paycheck; the very idea of being able to do what I wanted seemed beyond reach.

It's a cliché to say that passion is what makes life worth living. Like many clichés, it's also true. To care about the work you do, to be motivated by it, and to invest yourself in it is to feel every day that you are in the right skin and have found the right life for you.

In my corporate career, I knew from the get-go that I was in the wrong spot. So when my body itself reacted to my "career choice" in perspiration-soaked panic attacks, it wasn't a big surprise. In fact, the only thing that kept me going at all was the tradition of competitiveness that playing sports teaches you: the desire to win, the need to prevail, to hide failures, to cope, push through, endure.

Yes, I also needed to pay off my MBA debt and wanted to get to a place of financial stability. You know how that goes: "If I just keep making money, I'll eventually get to a place where I can do what I want." But by the time I was offered the gig on *The Bachelorette*, the *only* thing left of my career was the paycheck; the very idea of being able to do what I wanted seemed beyond reach.

What did I want to do? I probably couldn't have seen it myself back then, but I have always had a passion for the markets, specifically trading and investing—anything involved with analytics, including sports analytics for betting. I always regretted working for a bank where I couldn't keep an eye on the "action" on Wall Street during the day. Another passion is small businesses and especially start-ups, I think because I love the idea of leveling the playing field in finance and the business world so more people can enter.

My life today involves both of those passions. I have an investing app that people can use both to learn about investing and to do it. I also work with a number of small businesses on the rise, and I consult every day for hundreds of other people involved in all sorts of business. I also speak to organizations large and small about the importance of rewarding, educating, and engaging each and every employee; I've become something of an educator on the subject.

So, today, I am absolutely living my passion. The difference in my life between now and my ten years in corporate America could not be more sharp or more welcome.

Would another position or another company have saved me back then? Would it have freed me to get back in my own skin and love my work? It's not unlikely, and it's not important for our purposes. What matters is making the change that's right for you. Follow your passion, and you can't go wrong. I'm the living proof.

Changes

Jason Tartick @Jason_Tartick
I got here through this process of self-examination, which was essential in clarifying for me where I stood on each career determinant.

Maybe you're wondering what is different for me now that the handcuffs are off and I drink because I'm watching my Buffalo Bills romp to victory (or defeat) and *not* because I need to dull my emotions? The answer is: everything. Today, I work three times harder than I ever did—and don't pay attention to the clock. I'm excited every night to think about waking up the next morning, and when I wake up, I'm excited to get going, to do the work, to be with the people I get to work with. The handcuffs are off, I'm free, I've never been so involved in something that occupies me so completely, and I've never been happier.

I got here through this process of self-examination, which was essential in clarifying for me where I stood with each career determinant. It showed me that I at least understood my skill set issues and that I had a pretty sensible approach to my discontent about compensation. It spelled out for me that my mobility worries and my fear of the unknown were indeed holding me back from making a change, until the passion issue pushed me over the edge of my dissatisfaction and compelled me to make the change that, in my view, has saved my life. It also showed me that, in my case at least, the change was going to have to be radical.

Now it's your turn. You've talked to your friends, you've talked to your family, you've talked to yourself. Hopefully, you have also compared and contrasted their perception versus your reality. You've identified the issues that are the source of your career dissatisfaction and the issues that are keeping you from making the change you want to make. You now know which of the five issues point you to that change and define the nature of the change.

What lies ahead is the construction of a two-pronged strategic plan for each core issue. Unless you can snap your fingers and fly from your current job straight to the job that will answer all your demands (and I'm assuming you cannot), you probably have to stay in the job or career you now have so that you can continue to pay the bills until you're ready to make the break. That means you will need first an internal strategy aimed at keeping your boss happy and your employment assured—a strategy you will follow rigorously every hour of every workday. There are 168 hours in a week. In some of the many that remain after you have assured continuing employment, you will want to work on your external strategy, figuring out what excites you, what you really want to do in your life, what job or purpose will make you excited to get out of bed in the morning.

Yes, you'll need to be diligent with time management to do both tasks: one, meeting the expectations of the job you need to hold onto while two, working on the external strategy that will take you from your current reality to your restart. As you practice that diligence, I will be helping you strategize how to monetize where you want your restart to take you so that, in due course, you can detour sharply out of your current job and its dissatisfactions and into the career meant for you.

CHAPTER 3 RESTART REVIEW

All the Shit That's Fit to Stick

- ⮌ When building or rebuilding any structure, you need to start with the foundation; if it is flawed, the new structure simply won't stand.
- ⮌ Same thing in building a new way to make a living: you need to go deep into self-examination, right down to the bedrock of what isn't working for you.
- ⮌ You simply cannot restructure, reroute, or make the detour you want to make without peeling down to the core of the life and the career you're in right now. It starts with honesty and vulnerability as you ask yourself what's not working.
- ⮌ Skill set, compensation, mobility, fear, and passion are the five career determinants through which you can assess where you are, where you want to be, and how to get there.
- ⮌ You'll need to be diligent with time management to simultaneously meet the expectations of your job while working on the strategy that will take you to your restart.
- ⮌ You are a free agent. Stop giving companies the commitment they haven't given you.

4

Your Third-Degree Priority Probe

Where Should You Live?

*L*et's take a pause.

You've already been through three chapters digging into the thick of the process for getting yourself to a restart of your life and career. Specifically, you created at least a hairline fracture in the blueprint that was handed down to you. Then I hope you got vulnerable enough to tell yourself the raw truth about your life and career. And finally you developed a new definition of what constitutes a successful life—for *you*, on your terms and no one else's.

There's just one more thing you need to do now as you get ready to take specific, practical steps toward the restart you seek. Get your priorities straight. That's an old-time phrase people throw around a lot, often in the same way your mother told you to wear your warm coat in the winter or be careful driving. What I'm talking about, however, is a deep exploration into what is really most important to you. Deep and maybe difficult. And I am not going to use the same saying your mother or father did or any more old-time phrases. So, in my words: it's time to tighten your shit up! And let's do this right here, right now.

Call it Jason's Third-Degree Priority Probe. You know what I mean by "third-degree." It's the phrase that's used to describe the kind of interrogation cops and prosecutors carry out on suspects and witnesses, the kind of questioning that gets answers. Yes, I realize that many of *those* interrogations are completely fucked up, but what I am talking about is the strategy behind the questions asked. It's a strategy that backs you into a corner, forces you to look within, and insists that you find answers, potentially the answers you have been avoiding your whole life. I'm asking you to do a third-degree self-interrogation to determine what is really, really, really important to you in the one and only beautiful life you have been given.

To make it work, you'll have to stop giving a shit about what other people do—and certainly about what other people think of what you do. One of the things I began to realize the day after I lay shivering on the floor of the execs-only bathroom was that none of my colleagues or potential customers or any of the people who could influence my future were in there with me. None of my peers, whether friends or competitors or both at once, were with me when I was scarfing down anxiety pills or putting on an amiable-but-girded-for-action front when I stepped through the office door in the morning or going through the ol' Seattle Hair-gate Incident and actually changing my appearance because the bosses said, I "needed to fit the position." And I still can't stop thinking, "Remember when you dumbasses hired me with a $250,000-plus package when I had the same look and haircut you now want me to get rid of to 'fit the role'?" And after all that, like the sellout I had become, I cut my hair. But I digress.

When it came to the anxiety attacks, the pill taking, the hating myself for selling out, I was on my own. So why should I enable anyone but me to decide what really, really counts in my life?

Talk about work-life balance: the balance board can hold only one person at a time, so when it comes to staying upright on *my* life's balance board, I can't listen to anyone else's ideas. Neither can you.

We hear a lot about work-life balance in corporate America. Companies offer PTO—paid or personal time off, sometimes even unlimited PTO—as a sign that they get it. But let's be honest: most companies have moved to unlimited PTO so that they don't have to carry the liability of accrued PTO and pay you what you're due when you leave the company. As noted, with just about everything in corporate life, PTO has a cost. Maybe you cut back on vacation time to show your devotion to the job, and maybe PTO becomes just another passive-aggressive arena where your boss comments on how much vacation you have taken, even though you have earned that employee benefit. The truth is that no company can define your work-life balance, which makes the whole notion of PTO a bit of a joke. I could talk vacation-time bank, payout, and utilization strategies all day long, and I will do so later in this book, but for now, define work-life balance for yourself, and do it by my third-degree probe when you ask yourself what you prioritize in life.

I think a lot of people found themselves doing this kind of priority probing during the pandemic. Maybe because they were working from home and were therefore out of the "normal" work environment, and maybe because a health scare nearly always prompts the reminder that "you only live once," and maybe, too, because there was plenty of time to think about the long game, not to mention a flush of financial liquidity that suggested lots of possibilities. But whatever it was, a lot of people I know took a fresh look at their careers and lives while waiting out COVID-19.

That's good! It's healthy. And it's a reminder to all of us that the third-degree priority probe isn't a one-shot deal. It's something we should all do from time to time as a matter of habit, maybe by asking for a leave of absence to "clear the mind" or as something to undertake in the fresh surroundings of a vacation trip or as something we just stop and command ourselves to do from time to time precisely because we only live once and doing it happy and fulfilled is a lot better than the alternative.

In an interview I once did with *Shark Tank*'s Barbara Corcoran, as savvy and as entrepreneurial a businesswoman as there is, she revealed her process for undertaking any new project or enterprise. "My first step is I get a yellow pad, draw a line down the middle, and on one side I put what I love and on the other side I list what I hate. Then I figure out how can I make a career out of the things I love. That's my starting point."

Make it your *restarting* point. Use Barbara's love-and-hate list or just frame it this way: At the end of the day, what drives your individual pursuit of happiness? What is more important to you right now than anything else?

Is it financial gain with its promise of security and flexibility? Maybe it's professional advancement and the power and prestige of a place in the hierarchy and a say on executive matters. Or maybe for you it's strictly personal fulfillment through doing something you love with the right people around you in a place you want to be.

Yes, the answers will change over time, even day to day. Maybe your top priority now is to pay off your student debt once and for all. The desire to be out from under that obligation is the one thing you want more than anything else. And once it's paid, something else will take over as top of the list. But whatever *your* priorities are—not mine, not your parents', not those of your peers at the office, or of your bosses, or even of your significant other—those priorities will drive the essential decision making for building your life into what you want it to be: where you choose to live, what work you want to do, your financial goals.

And once you have done that third-degree probe of your priorities, you will be headed toward the pinnacle of your performance. The reason is simple: once you know what counts to you, your sense of excitement, your optimism, and your energy will naturally fire up what you do each day. And when excitement, optimism, and energy align with daily direction, the result is peak performance. Before Ken Jeong became the massive actor and comedian we know him to be, he was a licensed physician. Jeff Bezos was a computer scientist on Wall Street before he founded Amazon. Martha Stewart was a stockbroker before she became, well, Martha Stewart. Is the point I'm trying to make beginning to click? Those three, among many others, followed what counted to them. That decision fired up a kind of channeled energy whose power cannot be overstated. You can have such a restart, too, one based in and pegged to *your* priorities, a restart that will take you to the pinnacle of your performance and to a happy life that meets *your* definition of success.

A Place to Live

Between the ages of twenty-one and thirty, I relocated seven times to five states across a total distance of more than eight thousand miles. The longest of the relocations took me from Rochester, New York, to Seattle, Washington. None of those seven relocations include the three-month stint filming *The Bachelorette* when I lived in eight different locations: the Bachelor Mansion in Los Angeles, California; Park City, Utah; Las Vegas, Nevada; Richmond, Virginia; Nassau in The Bahamas; Buffalo, New York; Chiang Mai, Thailand; and home at the time, Seattle, Washington. All seven of those moves were work related; I was there because my job at the time required it, and that was my ass-backward sole priority.

While ass-backward, the moves grew out of a conscious decision precisely aligned with my priorities at the time, which basically were to rise up the corporate ladder and shoot up the pay scale as fast and as far as I could. I made it clear from the very beginning of my career in banking that I was "willing to relocate" because I knew that those words in the HR system or on a résumé or performance review were a plus in the eyes of management. So I went where they wanted me to go when they wanted me to go there. And I scored an uptick in my financial health with each move. The most significant relocation I accepted, the one to Seattle, also swept my title up to "senior" level. Another plus. But that wasn't the only reason I took the relocation; it wasn't even the real reason, because by then my priorities had changed significantly. So let me tell you why I actually took the gig three thousand miles away from my whole life to a place where I knew no one.

By the time the Seattle job came my way, I knew that what I wanted was to get out of corporate banking. I didn't yet know what I wanted to get into, but I did know that I would need money to find the answer. For me, that meant becoming debt free and saving up a good supply of cash to live on while I looked for that answer. The Seattle job was a two-year contract that I thought would enable me to pay my debts and build my savings so that I could afford to take the "leap of faith" I was hoping to find. I knew that I likely would not be a happy guy in Seattle, but I also knew that sticking with it would get me out; it would be worth it.

When *The Bachelorette* opportunity came up, I asked for a "personal leave of absence" from the Seattle job. The request was well thought out and strategic. When I submitted the request in the form of the deal memo, it was like a memo on fire, as I'll explain. See what you think.

Jason Tartick, MBA
VP, Senior Banking
Middle Market Banking

MEMORANDUM

The purpose of this memorandum is to request time off commencing March 12, 2018. The period of the requested time off may be as brief as five business days, returning to work on March 19, 2018, or as long as 35 business days, returning to work on Monday April 30, 2018.

I have accrued 192 hours, or 24 days, of Paid Time Off, 32 hours, or four days, of Sick Leave, and eight hours, or one day, of a Floating Holiday. Collectively, my Paid Time Off, Sick Leave and Floating Holiday total 29 days off.

Statistically, there is a 25% chance I will return to work after 5 days of PTO, 40% chance I will return to work after 10 days of PTO, 60% chance I will return after 15 days of PTO, 84% chance I will return after 20 days of PTO, and a 92% chance I will return in less than 30 days. While very unlikely, if my leave exceeds the allotted days off, I understand I will be placed on an unpaid leave of absence. I will return to work as soon my leave concludes.

To understand the basis of this unorthodox request, I would like to discuss what sparked this process. Gilda's Club Rochester, an affiliate of the Cancer Support Community, has been serving the Rochester, New York community since 1959, offering programs to men, women, teens, children and families who are affected by cancer. In March of 2017, I was sponsored by the Bank at the 8th Annual Gilda's Club Bachelor Auction. As a representative of the Bank and an active member of the Rochester community, I underwent an extensive interview process to be selected as one of "Rochester's Most Eligible Bachelors." The purpose of the Bachelor Auction was to raise funds leading up to the auction, with additional funds raised at the marquee event where each bachelor was auctioned off for a date. All proceeds benefitted Gilda's Club. With the Bank's sponsorship and support, I conducted interviews published in print, television, and radio media. I raised the most money going into the auction, the most money at the auction, and more money than any bachelor in the previous 7 years.

Several months after the event, I was approached and invited by the National Television Network, American Broadcasting Company (ABC) to be a participant in the television show "The Bachelorette." I am requesting this brief period of time off to take advantage of this once-in-a-lifetime opportunity to participate as one of the bachelors selected for the television show.

Since the age of 21, in June 2010, one month after graduating with my undergraduate degree, I began my service with the Bank. Since then, I have exceeded expectations each year, earning seven promotions within the retail, business banking, underwriting, and middle market groups. To further my career with the Bank and exhibiting my dedication to the company, I relocated four times, including Syracuse, Cleveland, Rochester, and Seattle. Furthermore, during my time at the Bank, I earned my MBA in accounting and finance from a top tier program to improve my skillset as a Banker here.

Since joining the Seattle team five months ago, I have developed credibility with my peers, clients, and prospects, resulting in a $2MM pipeline in income statement profitability. While I understand the unconventional nature of this request, I am hopeful that the Bank will be supportive throughout this venture. I have proven to the organization over almost eight years of unwavering commitment that I conduct myself professionally and represent my brand and the Bank's brand exceptionally well. Throughout this process, I will continue to uphold standards consistent with my character and the Bank's brand; and I am aware of the consequences for behavior that does not align with the Bank's brand.

With only limited time in the Seattle market, my client base is relatively small, so managing the open items and communication prior to my leave should be seamless. In preparation for this brief leave, I will put a plan in place for those open opportunities and services that will require attention in the one- to seven-week time frame.

I truly appreciate the magnitude and unusual nature of this request. I apologize for any inconvenience or distress my leave will cause. But, as I have dedicated almost the last decade developing and advancing my career entirely with the Bank, this brief leave to pursue growth within my personal life is important and a once-in-a-lifetime opportunity I cannot pass up.

Thank you for considering this request.

Sincerely,
Jason Tartick
Vice President /Senior Middle Market Banker

No one in the stiff-suited bureaucratic banking hierarchy wanted to sign off on that. It moved like it was on fire, barely touched by a couple of fingers before being passed on as fast as possible. So it went from my boss to the regional boss, to the president of the whole community bank who actually and weirdly enough immediately approved it. That was until an HR executive, familiar with the television show, stepped in and asked the president if he knew what he had just approved. He sure as hell didn't, but I was given approval to take a "personal leave of absence" so long as I didn't ruin my reputation on the show. Which meant I had nailed the leave of absence *and* had kept the terms of my two-year deal intact. So off I went to this bizarre new adventure, which turned out to change my life and to introduce me to people who became mighty important to me—fellow bachelors who became close friends, and above all, Kaitlyn Bristowe, who became much more than that in my life.

Being overly committed and overly loyal as an employee can come back to bite you.

Right after filming, which lasted only a quick three months, I of course moved back to Seattle and returned to work as a banker. As I noted earlier, the bank took advantage of my fifteen minutes of fame by using me as a kind of ambassador. They had me running charity events and presenting at networking luncheons where bank brass never failed to bring up my TV "experience." I appreciated that they had let me go on the show, so I saw all this as payback. For once, I felt like I had some leverage on them.

While working at the bank, I also began to accept freelance speaking engagements on the side, often on college campuses. And I undertook a number of brand sponsorships as well. It was a whole new ball game, an exciting and lucrative one, especially when I realized that my fee for a single Instagram post was more than my monthly paycheck. Hmm—this could change things!

But as I said earlier, being overly committed and overly loyal as an employee can come back to bite you. If you're a W-2 employee, the power is all in your employer's hands, not yours. Inevitably, all it took was one mishap for the bank to just drop me cold: one PG-13–rated, funny story about our sex life, not even made by me but by Kaitlyn on her podcast. A podcast that empowers hundreds of thousands of women weekly with the creed that we are all human, we all make mistakes, let's live on real truth and love who we are. You'd think a bank with a CEO who at the time was named *Forbes*'s number one most powerful woman in banking would have some appreciation for women-empowered podcasts. Nope. In fact, the appreciation was so minimal that the podcast had to be deleted from the network, costing Kaitlyn much more than my monthly salary. And boom! Just like that, my almost ten years of banking, seven relocations, and nine nearly perfect performance reviews meant nothing. I was out the fucking door!

Needless to say, I negotiated a fair exit plan (which we will address later), but it was clearly time to move. Where? Kaitlyn lived in Nashville, a city on the rise and almost as much connected with *The Bachelorette* as it is with country music. I was ready to flee Seattle. Where should we live that would meet both our sets of priorities?

The two of us are now in the marketing/entrepreneurship/media/entertainment worlds, the twin capitals of which are New York and Los Angeles. But Nashville is an up-and-coming leader in those fields as well and thus a good place to put down stakes for my new and growing career. Moreover, given the cost-of-living difference, we could live there much more comfortably for far less money than in either of those coastal cities. And as wild as it is, it's advantageous to live in a state without a state income tax. As of the writing of this book, Tennessee still is one of the nine states with no such tax.

In fact, the cost-of-living difference between Seattle and Nashville at the time came to 41 percent! It meant to me that if I took in $98,000 in annual income in Nashville, it would have been equivalent to making my $165,000 base salary in Seattle—a far costlier market. At the time, I could have made that $98,000 by taking on about six to nine speaking engagements, or executing three or four one-off Instagram post collaborations, rather than by sitting in an office, and I could wear my hair the way I wanted to and could maybe even work myself off the beta-blockers, Xanax, and SSRIs.

Note: cost-of-living adjustment obviously works the other way too. If I were making $500,000 in Nashville in 2018, do you know what I would have needed to live the same lifestyle in New York City? The answer is over $1.3 million.[1]

So Nashville offered both professional and financial advantage. We also had a circle of friends and associates there. And a big plus for me was that a move to Nashville could actually bring me closer to my family; it's a six-hour drive from where my parents now live and less than a two-hour flight to my brother and close friends in New York. Adding those personal advantages to the professional value *and* the gains in financial value effectively covered all the bases. Nashville with Kaitlyn, living very comfortably without financial pressure, being near family and with a growing circle of friends, and with all the resources available to carry out the work I wanted to do met all my priorities. Nashville is home.

Still, it's important to note that each relocation I undertook changed all sorts of things in my life, as I learned that where you live can determine how you live in so many ways. So it's worth remembering, as you carry out your careful consideration of the right place for your restart, that all kinds of changes are on the table. Will a small town supply the resources you need for your career and life choices? Will a big city overwhelm the kind of personal life you seek? If you choose to live in a place solely because of work, what secondary priorities are available or need to be confirmed? I'm talking about recreational resources, access to relatives, health care resources. If you choose to live in a place because it's near friends or family or the waterfront you love or your favorite ski slopes, will you easily be able to pursue the professional career you seek?

What drives the economy of where you choose to live? An economy fired by a smokestack industry may be good for your career but bad for your kids' health; a tech-based economy may smell sweet but add no value to your career plan. Of course, it may be that your career plan is to create a whole new economic engine that will thrust the place into overdrive. That's a good plan too.

But let's start the examination of where you should live with the most quantifiable of the issues to probe: money.

STEP 1:
The Sense and Dollars
Driving Where You Should Live

The fundamental question is whether where you live now is worth what you pay to live there and whether it provides financial earnings upside *in terms of your new definition of success.* The issue is the value rendered, measured in cost to earnings ratio. It's essential to define this value as precisely as possible once you have gone through your third-degree priority probe. When you have done that, you'll know whether or not your current location can deliver the financial value you seek. If not, that will prompt you to find the best place to consider moving to. Obviously, the best place will be the one where you can realize that value. Where can you get the success you have defined at a price that makes sense and that you can pay? Where can you get paid equitably and adequately for the skill set and value you offer?

To figure it out, you'll need to consider both financial factors and economic potential. The former begins with learning the costs of basic needs like food, shelter, transportation, energy, clothing, and health care, all of which are pretty easy to research. But don't forget about the desirable but not strictly essential items—the things that add to your quality of life. And by all means, remember to think about taxes at state and local levels. The resources list on page 62 and in the back of this book can point you to websites that keep abreast of all these costs and all taxes in the fifty states and in just about all US cities. You'll want to spend a bit of time figuring out what is pertinent to you, but the results will show you precisely how much you are paying for the financial value you're getting out of your current location or a potential future location.

If financial gain is your top priority, you also need to think about the acceleration of money. What place or places can best nourish that priority? I'm a living, breathing example of the reality that if you are willing to relocate, as I was early in my career, the acceleration of money is significantly magnified. Times were tough right after the 2008–9 financial crisis, but I landed a job right after graduating from college, I started my career at an annual salary of $40,000, and I let my company know that I would go anywhere. I estimate that eight years later, through my relocations and still with the same company, I realized a 650-plus percent financial return in my whole compensation package. If that kind of acceleration is a priority you want to pursue, be willing to move—and let your bosses know it; the willingness changes your status at once, and the moves boost the pace of your financial gain.

The COVID-19 pandemic made the opportunity of working remotely more common than ever in history. If the cost of living where you can work remotely is significantly cheaper than what the cost of living would be if you were required by your employer to work at a particular location, then the remote option becomes an opportunity to earn outsized income. An acquaintance working for a large financial corporation in New York City—and being compensated for New York's cost of living—in fact is working remotely in a more affordable and bigger house in upstate New York. He wins in every way: the comfort and space of living outside the big city, and the compensation due to someone living in the big city.

You also need to look at the overall economic strength of where you live now or of a location you may be considering. What are its growth prospects? Is there sufficient labor for future economic expansion, sufficient capital investment, room for and acceptance of entrepreneurship? Future projections are only that, but they can give you a sense of economic potential going forward.

Where can you find all this out? We all have our own ways of doing research, but again, the resources section in the back of this book is a good place to start. I've listed there a whole bunch of databases with both current data and projections of trends and possibilities, and I've also cited a number of assessments of "best" or "top 10" places to live if you're single, a newlywed, interested in a particular industry or a particular lifestyle, and much more.

You can figure out cost-of-living adjustments (COLAs) online. Here's a partial list of easy-to-access, easy-to-deal-with choices, plus a look at how fast and effective it can be to compare two locations:

SOURCES FOR COLA COMPARISON

- CNN: https://money.cnn.com/calculator/pf/cost-of -living/index.html
- NerdWallet Calculator: https://www.nerdwallet.com /cost-of-living-calculator
- SmartAsset Calculator: https://smartasset.com /mortgage/cost-of-living-calculator
- Bankrate Calculator: https://www.bankrate.com /calculators/savings/moving-cost-of-living-calculator .aspx
- Salary.com: https://www.salary.com/research/cost -of-living

As an example, using NerdWallet's version of a COLA calculator, it's easy to determine that if a person living in Nashville and enjoying a salary of $80,000 per year wants to move to San Francisco, the comparable salary there would be approximately $169,039. At the same time, the NerdWallet tool tells me that the person moving from Nashville would be confronting a different set of prices in San Francisco for key costs of living, as follows:

- Groceries: 29 percent more in San Francisco than in Nashville
- Housing: 288 percent more in San Francisco than in Nashville
- Utilities: 32 percent more in San Francisco than in Nashville
- Transportation: 55 percent more in San Francisco than in Nashville
- Healthcare: 39 percent more in San Francisco than in Nashville

But of course, when it comes to realizing your new definition of success, money is not the whole picture, even if financial gain is your top priority.

STEP 2:
Identify the Professional Value
You're Looking For in Where You Should Live

What value does a location bring to the new career you have in your sights? Put another way: Where on earth can you achieve your new definition of what constitutes personal success? Some professions, obviously, are location specific; you cannot operate a ski resort, much as you might love to, in Miami Beach. More subtly, you may live in a comfortably inexpensive city where the opportunity to gain a foothold in the industry you want to be aligned to is limited or nonexistent. Maybe you're in freelance website design, but the local college and chamber of commerce have a combined program to promote that skill set with locals trained in the required capabilities. That kind of setup could leave you out in the cold. By the same token, you may live in an expensive place where the industries that do provide opportunity add no value to your new idea of professional success.

Remember the $1.3 million–plus income I said I would need to live the equivalent of a $500,000 Nashville salary-sourced lifestyle if I moved to New York? An awful lot of people living in New York City maintain a lifestyle *waaay* below what $1.3 million can buy—and they wouldn't live anywhere else. The reason for that is another key component of where to live in order to ensure your definition of success. Some industries thrive in some places and not in others. If your personal success depends on one of those industries, being in the right place is absolutely essential for your success.

Right place, right time. It happens. As a kid growing up on the banks of the Ohio River in Kentucky, little Jennifer Lawrence always knew she wanted to be an actress, and while she performed regularly in school and church plays, she dreamed of the lights and action of New York and Broadway. When the Lawrence family traveled there on vacation—Jennifer was fourteen—a talent scout for a modeling agency spotted her on the street and photographed her. "I'll sign up for modeling only if I can act," she vowed to herself. She stuck to that vow, and that was it: she was on her way, slowly at first, to starring roles in blockbusters like *The Hunger Games*, to Oscars and BAFTA and Golden Globe awards, to phenomenal financial success, and to global admiration and influence. All from being spotted on a New York street by a guy with a great eye for beauty and a fine camera. Coincidence or fate, Lawrence was in the right place at the right time to virtually guarantee the career success she sought.

But to be in the right place for *your* career acceleration, you must decide if being where a particular industry "rocks" is a priority to you—the way Broadway and New York rock for theater people. There are websites aplenty that keep track of industry concentrations in particular geographic areas. That kind of concentration can be a plus but also a challenge. When I worked in banking in Seattle, I felt almost like a bum behind the technology industry that makes that city hum. That Seattle and its suburbs are home to the headquarters of both Microsoft (technically fifteen miles away in Redmond) and Amazon is only the beginning. The whole area is a hub of tech innovation and entrepreneurship—a tech and innovation ecosystem that has virtually redefined the whole region. If tech or anything related to tech is your dream, Seattle can be a paradise for professional advancement—if you can afford to live there. Its only real "competition" for growing the value of a tech professional career is San Francisco/Silicon Valley. As I write this, San Francisco is still some 20 percent more expensive than Seattle in terms of cost of living.[2] Still, the tech careerist trying to make up his or her mind between the two has a lot of thinking to do in comparing professional and financial opportunities. As a corporate banker, that kind of profession-related excitement just didn't exist for me.

STEP 3:
Identify the Personal Value
You Need in Where You Should Live

You already know that life isn't solely about the job or profession. Even if you're not someone for whom personal value is *the* top priority, we owe ourselves the value of personal happiness if we can make it happen. A good way to measure it in terms of your new definition of success is to ask this simple question: For you to be happy, what do you need readily available to you?

For most of us, the answer is people: friends, congenial neighbors, family nearby or accessible in some way.

For many of us, a fulfilling job with time and opportunity for other "extracurricular" activities is more than enough.

But for each of us, there are other quality-of-life elements that we find important, perhaps even essential, to our ability to live a rich and happy life. So it's crucial to research those elements to ensure that they exist in the place, are accessible, and are real enough to meet your needs.

Only you can determine if the place you live or are considering moving to satisfies those personal needs—sufficiently, pretty well, well enough, or perfectly. And only you can decide whether sufficiently, pretty well, or well enough will work for you. I will never forget kidding around with my brother after he and his husband bought a home on Manhattan's Upper West Side. I was kind of taunting him. "Steven," I said, "I just pulled up a home in Nashville, Tennessee, that would be a monstrous mansion for what you paid for your home in that city. Custom-designed!" Again, he lived up to that blueprint-breaker mentality he had since he was a kid. I will never forget his response: "Oh, a customized mansion. Sounds cool, I guess. But . . . I would then live in Nashville, Tennessee, and not New York City. So thanks but no thanks!" For him, the personal happiness he and his husband find in living in that exact place is the priority. The cost, size, or grand design isn't the priority, because his third-degree priority probe defined the location of his residence as core to personal happiness.

Seattle is a fantastic city. It has great food, great culture, music, restaurants, and shops. It offers proximity to beautiful outdoor locations. It is a sports-nutty town. It has all sorts of things I love.

But I didn't know a soul there. Propelled by a fantastic promotion, I arrived, settled down to work—and possibly spent so much time working that I never really got around to making friends, other than one colleague at the bank, Nate, who is still a good friend. I told myself that the city's vibe was different from what I was comfortable with, but the truth is I was so accustomed to being around people I knew well and for a long time that I just wasn't as dedicated as I might have been to seeking people out and getting to know them. And I guess I never realized the extent to which having those people in my "past life" generated an energy, optimism, and excitement that powered a lot of my overall success and happiness. There just wasn't enough of it for me in Seattle. For that reason, I rate Seattle's personal Jason Tartick value at $0.00. Maybe even negative!

Finding personal value can be an engine of your success. Not finding it can have just the opposite effect. If a location doesn't ensure that you can find and enjoy the things that are important to you, then no amount of money and not even the world's most perfect job will bring you the satisfaction you are looking for.

You can't effectively restart your
life and career until you
understand the value of both.

I started this chapter by suggesting you take a pause long enough to carry out a third-degree probe of your financial, professional, and personal priorities. It's been a chance to rethink and possibly reposition yourself in terms of a place to live. You can't effectively restart your life and career until you understand the value of both to the place where you live, and then, based on the priorities your third-degree probe has revealed, to either recognize it's time for a move or acknowledge you're already in the best place for a successful life. Whether you stay or relocate, make sure it's those personal priorities that shape where you choose to live.

And once you've done that, it's time to talk about a new job and, specifically, how to "streamline" the hiring process.

CHAPTER 4 RESTART REVIEW

All the Shit That's Fit to Stick

- Jason's Third-Degree Priority Probe is a strategy that backs you into a corner, forces you to look within, and insists that you find answers to the questions you have been avoiding.
- Once you know what counts to you, your sense of excitement, your optimism, and your energy will naturally fire up what you do each day.
- Being an overcommitted and overly loyal employee can come back to bite you. If you're a W-2 employee, the power is all in your

employer's hands, not yours. One mishap and you could be out
the door.

🔁 Conduct a third-degree probe of your financial, professional, and
personal priorities.

🔁 As you think about the right place for your restart, all kinds of
changes are on the table, including relocating. Small town? Big
city? You'll need to identify the financial, professional, and
personal value of where you want to live.

5

Your Career Cure

Crystalizing the Core Pillars of Your Career!

y now, it's normal to feel like you're kicking your own ass. I have asked you to rethink everything: the system you were brought up in, the life you're living every workday, and hell! I have even asked you to rethink every aspect of the place you call "home" and, more specifically, to consider whether the fact that you call it home even makes any sense! By now, you've done a good bit of reversing, retracing, and rewiring.

You've also defined what are to you the pillars of a successful future—the one or more determinants that you want to shape the career you seek.

And hopefully you've gone in hard on yourself, given the third degree to your priorities, putting them through the most uncompromising kind of grilling to identify the ones that stand up to every challenge. The aim of all this tough self-questioning has been to sharpen your ability to identify what your next career move will be.

So the next key question, based on all that you've learned or confirmed about yourself, is: What are your options for a restart that will get you to the future you seek, one built on what you have determined are the pillars of a fulfilling career, by which I mean a career that fulfills *your* priorities?

The only way to see those options is through the lens of how *you* define career success. No other standard makes sense. So, in this chapter, let's take a look at how to line up the options that can get you out of the stall you're in and move you forward. I'll go through all five of the essential career determinants we covered in chapter three and will outline the alternative courses of action each pillar suggests. If the course of action you take doesn't begin in what you now know defines career success for you, it won't be worth the journey. Trust me when I tell you: getting this shit right doesn't happen overnight. It's a grind, but if you don't put the *work in now*, you will always look back at your career wondering "what if?" or worse, "if only . . ."

We'll do this one pillar at a time. Here's why: you know which pillar you consider the most important and the most valuable to the career you seek. You know which pillar is least important to you. Rank the ones in the middle as well so that you have a full appraisal of just how valuable each pillar is to the fulfillment of your career ideal. That will be the basis of a plan for lining up your options in the right order as well.

Compensation

Jason Tartick @Jason_Tartick
If you're not negotiating every
single day of your life, you're not negotiating enough.

If you're one of those folks who learned from the self-examination of chapter two that the reward of being paid is the main pillar of your career (and it's a popular and pretty common choice), I have good news for you. It is the easiest career determinant to fix and requires the least amount of time. That's because if compensation is what counts for you, you have only two options: either find ways to earn higher compensation doing the same trade or work, or find other ways to make more *outside* your existing job. Or, hell, I'll add a third option: do both! The fix is easy, and it's one you can take on right now.

I love the definitions of the word *compensation*. I'm told that if you go back to the original Latin, it literally means to weigh two things together, one against the other. So, compensation is some-thing given to make up for something else. It's the monetary re-ward you get if you've been injured in an accident or, of course, the monetary value paid to us employees in exchange for the work we do. If it is for you the prime determinant of career success—and if you have a clear understanding of the earning potential within your line of work—then you may not have to change your job or move to another industry. Based on earnings potential, your best option may be to just get yourself a raise.

It will take some work. The uncomfortable discussions must now become comfortable. You will need to know how to quan-tify your worth, and you will need to know how to ask and advo-cate effectively for what you want. Unfortunately, we all live in a world where we must self-promote; if you can't sell yourself and your value, you will have difficulty earning what you are worth.

When I was first being considered for the Bachelor role, I was told it was between Blake Horstmann, Colton Underwood, and me. I knew that this was something I really wanted to do. Now, of course, compensation was part of the process, and the fact is that each of us was offered $100,000. I obviously knew that was what *I* was offered, but how did I learn the others were offered that as well? I asked them, and they told me and even showed me the contract. We were each offered $100,000 to be the Bachelor on Season 23.

Yet I knew that the long-term value of this gig to me personally was so much greater than the monetary value alone, which is why I was very close to going to the producers and telling them I would do the show for nothing. For all sorts of reasons that I bet you can understand, it was the position that was important to me. "Reverse negotiating" my contract and dropping the money part could have been a differentiator in what was a highly competitive process. I didn't reverse negotiate, and I am almost certain it wouldn't have worked, but I bring it up here because it's the exact opposite of compensation as a determinant of career success. For me at that time in that circumstance, compensation was just not that important; I actually thought about making noncompensation a strategy toward closing the job I so badly wanted.

But let's get back to those of you for whom compensation is the key determinant of success, the pillar on which you want to build your career.

Start by understanding that compensation is far more than salary. It is a total package comprising what can be a wide range of benefits: pension plan, stock purchase plan, equity, a signing bonus, base salary, vacation time, health insurance, health savings account allocations, disability insurance, life insurance, 401(k) match, possible car allowance, possible business-expense stipend. With more people working remotely, compensation might even include the ability to expense office or computer supplies or to subsidize a portion of your rent or mortgage.

Add to this a clear statement of your job title and job grade, the salary band your job occupies, and whatever other "creative" new jargon classifications your company comes up with. You likely will have to deal with the HR department to learn the stated minimum and maximum salaries of your current job title and grade, and certainly one of the things you will want to negotiate if you plan to stay with the company is a higher maximum as part of the raise you're seeking. (By the way, if you do decide to move to another company, negotiate to start there at a higher title and grade than the one you hold at the job you're leaving. That will help jump your future raises in the new company and beyond.) As for negotiating, that is of course a whole other animal we will tackle in a later chapter. But be aware that if you're not negotiating every single day of your life, you're not negotiating enough. Almost every discussion you have with another human personally, professionally, or financially contains some component of negotiation.

Back to your total package of benefits, title, and grade: it is what you now need to evaluate. Attach a value to each one of these moving parts. To do so, benchmark your package against other companies that directly and indirectly compete with yours. I told you back in chapter two how, in order to define the salary I wanted, I reached out to a bunch of recruiters looking for bankers, snowed them with my résumé and performance reviews, and asked each to make me an offer. That's an excellent way to find your market value and therefore to evaluate the package you want from your company. Stack yourself up against the competition so you can let your company know what others say you're worth. Plow through the internet as well. Check out blogs where people disclose this information or look for benchmarks on such job-search websites as glassdoor.com, comparably.com, Blind, and others where you can research compensation trends and facts.

Talk to your peers. Talk to your superiors. I know: nobody wants to talk about compensation. In corporate America, it "just isn't done," as if discussing how much money you're making or want to make were a dirty little secret not discussed in polite circles. To that I say, "Bullshit!" It's total and complete nonsense. It's a mechanism that gives us, the employees, less information when negotiating against the giant. When I was in business school, there was another guy in my program. We grew up in the same town, went to the same elementary school, same middle school, same high school, same college, had similar work experience and similar income, and were now in the same B-school. We both got accepted and were performing at similar levels, but through conversation with him, I found out that his scholarship was 10 percent bigger than mine.

That sent me right through the door of the scholarship office where I made my case, pointed out the comparisons, and leveraged the whole thing into a similar scholarship with the exact same percentage as his. Believe me, on a $100,000-plus tuition, a few percentage points of scholarship money can make a big difference, and the key to gaining it was my insistence on talking about money and pointing out that equal qualifications merit equal scholarship. On an episode of my podcast, *Trading Secrets*, I interviewed Mister Wonderful, aka Kevin O'Leary, and directly from the shark's mouth: "Tell everybody what you are making, and then you will find out in your social circles who is overpaid and who is underpaid. Then figure out what you're worth. You totally disclose that as it is part of the negotiating process."

So take everything you have learned and your careful analysis of your worth, go meet with the higher-ups—not just your boss, but your boss's boss, and even his or her boss—and sell it. Make your case. Show them what you have achieved from a performance perspective and spell out—or count out—the significant monetary value you have created for them. Earn the amount you seek by snowing them with the power of the value you bring.

And when the circumstances call for another raise, do it all over again.

Is Asking for a Raise a Tough Thing to Do?

JUST 37 PERCENT of workers have *ever* asked for a raise from their current employer.

Hello? Did you catch that? Not quarterly, not biannually, not annually, but little more than a third of all workers have *ever* asked for a raise according to data published by payscale.com. The male-female gap in asking for a raise is negligible, with 37 percent of men and 36 percent of women saying they have asked. The difference comes in getting the raise: 82 percent of men get a yes answer versus 74 percent of women, according to a report in marketplace.org. And Glassdoor reports that to get those raises, women pretty much have to ask for raises bigger than what men get, then settle for dollar amounts equal to those of men. These numbers are so telling of so many issues! As for wanting to get paid, we outline a strategy for that in a future chapter.

Mobility

Jason Tartick @Jason_Tartick
Are you confident that your company is looking out for you and the track you are on? Are you confident it's even paying any attention to you?

Answer this question I'm borrowing from a well-known firm that shall remain nameless: If I were to offer you a pile of cold, hard cash right now to leave your job, would you take the money and run? If you answer yes, you probably sense that rising up the career ladder is an issue in your current organization; that it is not a company that is working hard to create viable, expansive growth and career paths for its employees. On the other hand, this firm, which again shall remain nameless, is so committed to its employees that it offers that exact proposition to all employees posttraining: the equivalent of one month's salary, just to leave. The managers of said company have recognized the importance of their employees and know that the cost of turnover is too gruesome to pay. Companies like that exist, so why settle for those that don't!

But let's drill down further. Are you confident that your company is looking out for you and the track you are on? Are you confident it's even paying any attention to you? That's what mobility and the chance for career elevation come down to. At base, it's about your opportunity to act freely and proactively on behalf of your own future. In my view it's what enables autonomy, the chance to act as you see fit and to grow in the company with both your capabilities and your freedom intact. It's the exact opposite of a running theme during my almost ten corporate years: feeling like you are in career jail from Monday morning through Friday and just counting down the time!

Yet things like the following happen all the time in corporate America: You make a great point in a meeting, and your boss shoots it down, then sends out a memo claiming it as his idea, or hell! Maybe he presents it at the big meeting with the top dogs and you don't even know about it. A staffer in corporate communications works like hell to research and write a report on a key topic, and the up-and-coming manager she wrote it for submits it as his "final paper" for Harvard's Executive Leadership summer school! You report on a problem you've been asked to solve; nobody listens, nothing gets solved. Wild how plagiarizing a college paper can result in expulsion, but at some corporate giants, plagiarism will put you on the fast track. I witnessed these and similar examples daily during my time in the corporate world.

Maybe you have as well. Stories like this are as old as freaking dirt. They are the soft underbelly of many corporations, and if rising up the career/title/pay-grade ladder is a key determinant of career success for *you*, it's essential to make sure your company is serious about helping you do it. Is it serious about employee engagement and retention, about looking out for your best interests, and giving you objective, measurable, and transparent reasons to stay loyal?

The questions to ask are pretty simple: Does your company and its leadership focus on employee growth? Is the company committed to putting you and others like you in the best position to succeed there?

If not, the lack of upward mobility for you in the job you now have is likely an issue. You may just be in the wrong department in the company. If so, one solution is to find a way to have conversations with people in other departments and with their bosses. But if that doesn't solve the issue, then even with everything else aligned well, you're simply in the wrong company, and your best option is to leave.

Do it carefully. Spend the time and effort needed. Begin by looking at the company's direct competition and keep looking until you find a replacement company or companies where employee growth is a top priority. The kind of companies that pay people to leave.

Skill Set

Jason Tartick @Jason_Tartick
Which of your skills are working hard? Which are being ignored? Which are getting no exercise at all?

Remember my story about Barbara Corcoran and her twenty-two failed jobs by the age of twenty-three? What in the living hell?! But wait a minute, there must be a lesson here. Maybe one reason Barbara moved on, then moved on again, then moved on again and again was that each of those twenty-two jobs added something to her ever-growing skill set. Maybe she was taking from each of those dead-end jobs what could add to her portfolio of skills, leaving the dead ends behind her, and constructing a skill set that she would apply with stunning success to one of the toughest and most competitive businesses there is: New York City real estate. (Could this be why her autobiography is titled *Use What You've Got*?) Or maybe Barbara just went through a wildly accelerated process of identifying where her natural skill set was best deployed.

In your chapter three self-examination, you were tasked to define the precise skill set that makes you uniquely you. That exercise told you your specific, very own value—the strengths that differentiate you. I'm assuming you understood that meant both the hard skills you labored to master such as technical expertise, analytical proficiencies, and the things you got a degree or certificate for, plus the soft skills that come naturally to you, like teamwork, interpersonal communication, flexibility, motivation, or whatever your strengths may be.

The truth is that if you try on a skill set that is *not* uniquely you, it just won't work. I found that out back when I was feeling unhappy in my job and was looking for something new and different. I had an MBA, and I had banking experience. One of the obvious paths for that combination was the world of private equity, the alternative investment class that invests directly in private companies or in buyouts of public companies. It's pretty much considered the top of the totem pole in the world of finance, but I figured I had the chops and should give it a try.

As a guy from a regional bank, not a national institution, and as a non–Ivy Leaguer, I knew it would be tough to find my way into the private equity world—which typically recruits the top-tier graduates from Harvard, Wharton, Tuck, and the like. But I activated my network and eventually got connected—through my brother, actually—with an established businessman and my brother's father-in-law, Rick Schneidman, who got me an interview with two partners of The Jordan Company, a prominent New York firm.

Let me put it this way: sitting down with two partners of The Jordan Company in their corporate headquarters was a very, very big deal for me. There was no way I could ever have gotten the attention of executives like this without Rick—and no way I could have gotten to Rick without working my network.

So that's what got me there, and as prepared as I was—having rehearsed endlessly in my head exactly what I wanted to present—I was definitely nervous when we shook hands and they asked me to sit down.

"Tell us about yourself," the older partner said to me.

And I did. I told them exactly what I do and how I do it, and I assured them, articulately and persuasively, that the skills I could bring to The Jordan Company would make a significant difference. I was pretty sure I had achieved everything I had set out to do in my presentation, and I honestly believed I had nailed the interview.

That's when they started to laugh.

"You're a talented guy," the younger partner said to me, "but let us put you through a brief exercise." He dialed his assistant and asked if she could bring two senior analysts into the interview.

"All right, Jason," the partner said to me. "This is the role we would slot you in, and here are two guys in the role, so ask them whatever you want to know about our work here."

So I asked a few questions, the guys answered them, and the partner dismissed them.

Now the older partner took over again. "We see who you are," he said to me. "We caught your energy, and we see that you're someone who will go out there, find business deals, build a network, get the deals done, execute the deals."

He pointed to the door that had just closed on the guys I had questioned. "But you are not *those* guys," he said to me, "and those guys are not *you*. Those guys are desk jockeys. They sit still for twelve to sixteen hours a day. They analyze numbers, they build models, they work Excel from morning to night.

"It would take years of your being in that position—and other analytical positions—before you could be doing what you do best, which is building business and finding deals. I can put you in that position—no problem. But I genuinely don't think you'd be happy in it, because based on this past hour of talking to you, the incredible skill sets you *do* possess will not serve you well in a 'sit-still-and-analyze' desk jockey position."

That was an important interview for me. It taught me to listen to my inner autopilot, and it gave me clarity about the skill set I really do have.

After that, the only question I had to ask myself is the question you should be asking yourself right now: Does your skill set align with the daily requirements you face for meeting or exceeding expectations in the work you do under the title your company gave you and operating under the set of guidelines the company has established? It's a long question but basically a simple one: Which of your skills align well with the work assigned to you and which are underused or just not in the picture? The answer is in the alignment. Think about it: Are you going to find either career satisfaction or personal fulfillment if you leave your best shot outside the office door when you go to work in the morning? If your unique skill set doesn't align with the work you're doing, you are wasting your time and the boss's money.

You want to know what avoiding misalignment looks like? It's *Shark Tank*'s Daymond John resisting peer pressure and not getting sucked into the drug-dealing that was a core business in the neighborhood in which he grew up. Instead, backed by his loving and indomitable mother, Daymond "listened" to his individual skill set. Starting out with wool ski hats and T-shirts while working shifts at Red Lobster to keep things going, he put this ingenuity for fashion to work and founded FUBU, now a global retail empire with more than $6 billion in sales.

How about Erika Nardini? The chief marketing officer of AOL left the corporate grind to head Barstool Sports, at the time a what-the-hell start-up digital media company aimed at producing content on sports and pop culture. What-the-hell indeed: Nardini swapped the I-can-do-this-in-my-sleep "processing plant" that was the AOL service provider for an exciting, creative shot at developing a fresh-thinking, unconventional, mixed-media monster.

Under Erika's management, the monster has taken the internet by storm with more than two hundred employees and a valuation on the way to $1 billion as this book goes to press.

Then there's my personal favorite, my fiancée—hitched as of 2022—Kaitlyn Bristowe. In her late twenties she felt lost and depressed, was using painkillers, and was actually living in her parents' basement. Fast-forward a few years to today, and this former Bachelorette is a winner of *Dancing with the Stars*; host of *Off the Vine,* a top podcast across North America; founder of Dew Edit Hair Accessories; and founder of Spade and Sparrows Private Wine Label. Kaitlyn has even added the role of cohost of *The Bachelorette* to her extensive résumé of successes. "I did it very scared, but I did it," says Kaitlyn. Yes, it can be scary to realign yourself and your skill set, but just look at the change it created for her! Getting comfortable with the uncomfortable can pay massive dividends.

If you are looking for a restart because your skill set is not clicking with your career, it's not your skill set that needs changing. It's your career! Restarting requires a mindset that won't accept the status quo but challenges you to think in new ways. There simply is no future in a career in which you are "throwing away your shot" every day. If that sounds like you, start looking for restart options in areas where your skill set aligns with the actual work.

For example, maybe your expertise in financial analysis aligns full-time with the daily requirements of your current job, but what you see as your strong capabilities in organizational design are just not getting a workout at all. And that's too bad, because the numbers you're so good at are showing you that the workflow dysfunctions in the organization are growing worse. That's bad news for the organization, but it is really bad for you and for your ability to achieve the career success you crave. The answer is to get out of that present position and find where and how you can apply your full skill set maximally to achieve and surpass expectations.

That's the only way you can arrive at the pinnacle of what should be your professional journey.

And it opens a number of options. It could mean you're in the wrong job, the wrong organization, or the wrong industry. Maybe you *own* the wrong company. You built it, but the way it's working now, it is not letting you optimize your specific, you-defining skill set to achieve the success you want.

On the other hand, it could mean you're just in the wrong slot or the wrong department of an organization. Say you're a recruiter in the HR department, where there are typically multiple functional areas: benefits, compensation, labor relations, compliance, and talent management in addition to recruiting. As you look hard at the skill set that is not aligning with the people-oriented job you now do, you just might find that your particular, differentiating set of capabilities would work well in organizing and piecing together the metrics, reports, and data analytics needed in HR compliance. If that's the case, move over to the compliance function and leave recruiting to others.

Remember that no one who has achieved professional excellence did it without ensuring that their natural and earned skill sets were aligned with their day-to-day responsibilities. If skill set alignment is the core issue of your career dissatisfaction, keep meeting expectations at work, but start building your plan to find the right alignment of your skill set to your career and the work you're doing. And here's a tip: before you take a full leap out of your day job, you might think about taking on some side hustles as a potentially lower-risk alternative for finding your natural skill set.

Fear

Jason Tartick @Jason_Tartick
There's no way around it: being in a career and being afraid of what's next absolutely sucks.

What are you afraid of? The unknown, of course. That probably includes tomorrow when your schedule looks horrific. Will you get through tomorrow? You will. After all, you got through today.

Will you succeed in this career? Will you succeed as well as your classmates, who, to hear them tell it, are succeeding by leaps and bounds? Will you succeed as well as your sister or brother, your cousin or best friend?

Maybe worse, if you don't succeed, will that be okay with you? Will you have any priorities left over from that third-degree probe you did in chapter four that may be able to fill the void? After all, being afraid is supposed to be a driver of a great career. Don't they tell you that the door marked "fear" is the one you have to walk through to success?

Without a doubt, complacency would be a lot more comfortable than the fear you're living with. You would plug along each day at the job, and your expectations would never veer out of range of "a job is a job, and it pays the rent." But you can't seem to get into that groove or to stop thinking about what tomorrow may bring and worrying about whether you'll be ready for it. I could tell you that nobody is ready for what tomorrow brings, but you won't believe it, and you'll be right. There's no way around it: being in a career and being afraid of what's next absolutely sucks.

But one thing I can do is share a lesson I learned from my MBA professors about market efficiency. The market is efficient to the degree to which its prices reflect all the information that is relevant and available as well as information not available but that still plays into the market. Therefore, no one investor can have an advantage over another; all of the information determining whether a stock is undervalued or overvalued, underpriced or overpriced is available and baked into the price. There is also no way to "beat" the market because the real-time information is already reflected in it. That's the theory of market efficiency.

I like to transfer that to the efficiency of being human. Human survival, like the market, reflects all the information that is relevant and available about each of us, and therefore about you. Your brain contains all the instincts and information developed from birth: the time you took a fall as a little kid and got back up, thus teaching yourself to try not to fall, all the way to those tests you failed or teams you were cut from and how somebody sweet and loving helped you feel better about it. That same brain is brilliantly equipped to bring all those skills to the fore when needed.

So there are two things you need to do if you fear for your future. The first is to tell yourself that being born healthy and with a brain is the ultimate gift. Try to put it to use. One way to use it is to remind yourself that people on their deathbeds tend not to regret what they did in life but what they did *not* do. Recall the priorities your third-degree probe revealed one more time—maybe recite them aloud every morning and every evening. Remember how you learned not to fall and not to be destroyed by deep unhappiness.

Second, make sure your career "insurance" is up to date. Check your CV or résumé, your list of contacts, your accreditations and licenses, portfolio of work, your website, social media profiles, letters of recommendation, reference list—all the building blocks of a professional profile. Be certain everything is in order, up to date with current data, and ready to be accessed at any moment. It means that if you really do need to make a change, you're equipped and ready. The feeling of career fear can become a comfortable kind of complacency, but it is far from fulfilling. Break the status quo of your day-to-day job routine and break free of the fear.

Passion

Jason Tartick @Jason_Tartick
When I listened to me and only me, I knew it was time
for a leap of faith.

No one wants to live without passion, and no one should. No one
wants to live a life in which the passion isn't freed up till you walk
out the office door in the evening, then gets tied up again when
you walk back through that door in the morning.

Let's face it: we spend most of our life at work. To live that
time without excitement, without the desire to dream bigger,
without the energy to broaden our vision and aspirations is just
not worth it. The lack of passion in my life was the reason I
chucked a ten-year career, the big bucks, and certain future "stability" to take my chance on a reality TV show. That's what it
took for me to find my passion, and that of course is the essential
purpose of a two-option strategy to bring passion and true success to your life's work.

At the time, I was the only person I knew who needed to find
their passion. My parents were bewildered! How could you throw
this all away? For a dating show? Hell, they would have bought me
a lifetime membership on match.com if only I told them I was
going to stay in my career grind and not go on *The Bachelorette*.
But I just couldn't do it. I could not keep up the Monday-to-Friday
front of "all is okay" while feeling totally unfulfilled. It's why I've
been begging you from the outset: listen to *you*, not to the system
that created you or to the blueprint you were supplied with at
birth. When I listened to me and only me, I knew it was time for
a leap of faith. Even if it meant I was "throwing almost ten years
of work out the window." It beats throwing away a lifetime of being stuck in a passionless profession.

But while there is no longevity for you in work that does not trigger your passion, there is no particular advantage in quitting your job cold turkey. So one option is the strategy I call the 4V5—aka the shorthanded option. I call it that because hockey is a game I love and played growing up in Buffalo, and for those who don't know, being shorthanded in hockey means that the other team has one more player on the ice than your team has: four players versus the standard five. A certain kind of skill set is required for the 4V5; the players have to dig, grind, hustle, stop and start, keep their sticks active, get big, get wide, go as aggressive as possible, using every single square foot of ice and cutting every angle so that, working as a group, the combined strength of four players equals the sum of your opponent's five.

The 4V5 shorthanded option is what I'm asking you to undertake as you stay in your current situation while simultaneously searching for your next career move. You'll need to spread yourself thin yet remain disciplined with the use of your time and energy. Keep on paying the bills and meeting those job expectations as you grind away. No, it's not hockey you're playing; it's the tough game of life, and you've got to play it so hard that if *feels like* you're one player short and it's up to you to make up for that as you explore your options for finding your passion and blending it with your career.

That exploration of options will require a process of serious, steady self-scrutiny. You will ask yourself what brings true pleasure to your existence, what you really value, what triggers your excitement, and what you dream about experiencing in your time on earth. All of this will require talking to recruiters, networking, branding yourself, identifying potential industries, and researching companies. Yes, you need to do all this at the same time that you are grinding out the current job, till you are eventually ready to move from shorthanded to even—and ultimately to the moment you get your shot on the power play.

The power play is the dream. When you're on it, it's your world and the other team is living in it. You are playing for a period of time with one more player than your opponent. Now it's a 5V4 in *your* favor. The power play becomes the time of transition in your career journey. On a day-to-day basis you will transform the grinding efforts of shorthanded 4V5 into the composure, finesse, and creativity of 5V4. You will go from being at a disadvantage to having the advantage. You're holding onto your current job while you know what you need to do to get to an even playing field. Then you take the power play to that even field and turn the answers you've found into a career that scores the win and pays off in every way.

THE SHORTHANDED 4V5	THE 5V4 POWER PLAY
Penalties happen—in hockey and in life. When they come your way in hockey, it means you have to play with one less team member. That's four skaters doing the work of five—which is no time to be stagnant. The same goes for restarting your life and career.	*You're up and you're feeling great—but the grind doesn't stop there. Keep on your toes and keep growing even if you're in an ideal situation by focusing on these aspects of your development.*
• Manage Your Time Actively	• Enhance Your Skill Set
• Analyze Your Current Situation & Goals	• Magnify Creativity
• Network Daily	• Scale Proactively
• Build Your Brand	• Become an Expert
• Research the Industry	• Drill Down on Pointed Research
• Analyze Companies	• Develop Soft Skills
• Benchmark Compensation	• Build on Positive Momentum
• Do Your Location Due Diligence	• Sharpen Day-to-Day Expectations
• Apply, Apply, Apply	• Increase Goals

If that sounds like a lot of work, it well may be, but as I've also noted before, the workweek is 40 hours; that still leaves 128 hours every week. And what could be more important than spending that time finding your passion and figuring out how to make it pay?

Do you know about the college dropouts Francesca Mariano and Maria Ciuffo? Maybe you know them better as Fran and Ria, creators and hosts of the *Chicks in the Office* podcast (through Barstool!). Ria quit the famed Fashion Institute of Technology, while Fran left Georgetown even though both her parents are Georgetown alums. Talk about breaking a blueprint and upending expectations!

They never ended up going back to college because Barstool Sports is where they wanted to be. What they wanted to do was to become the go-to source for what's what and who's who in pop culture. Which is exactly what *Chicks in the Office* does every day. As I write this, Fran and Ria boast a social media following of 1.5 million listeners, trigger a million page views a week, and enjoy a level of financial rewards beyond anything they had ever dreamed of.

Yet, in their eyes, what really counts is that they love going to work in the morning, love what they do, and wouldn't be anywhere else or doing anything other than what they're doing now. From college students to interns at a start-up to renowned hosts of an internationally known show, a couple of college kids found a way to break the blueprint and join their passion to the very human need to work. Not bad for a couple of dropouts! They did it their way, against the will of most of the people advising them, and to this day, they say it's the best decision they ever made!

There's really no other option for a restart if passion is the pillar of career success you seek.

Find your passion. Ask yourself what excites you. Discover what you really love. Dedicate yourself to this task, then find the job and the company that will give you the opportunity to turn your passion into a career. That is the career in which you are bound to succeed.

CHAPTER 5 RESTART REVIEW

All the Shit That's Fit to Stick

- Compensation is the easiest career determinant to fix and requires the least amount of time. If that's what counts for you, either find ways to earn higher compensation doing the same work or find other ways to make more outside your existing job.

- If your company and its leadership don't focus on employee growth, the lack of upward mobility for you is likely an issue.

- It's critical for your skill set to align with the daily requirements of your job. Which of your skills are working hard? Which are being ignored? Which are getting no exercise at all? The answer is in the alignment.

- Remember that people on their deathbeds tend not to regret what they did in life but what they did *not* do. Make sure your career "insurance" is up to date. Check your résumé, your list of contacts, your accreditations and licenses, portfolio of work, and letters of recommendation—the building blocks of a professional profile.

- No one wants to live without passion, and no one should. But while there is no longevity for you in work that does not trigger your passion, there is no particular advantage in quitting your job cold turkey. You'll need a longer-term strategy for that.

6

Hacking the Hiring Process

*I*n case you hadn't figured it out by now, I am all about tearing down those "standard" practices that work against us so we can get them working *for* us. At this point in thinking about restarting your career and your life, you are probably ready for the hiring process. I hope you're looking forward to it with some zeal. So, in this chapter, as its title suggests, we will overturn standard practices in the hiring process with the simple aim of "correcting" that process—step by careful step.

To begin, let's shoot down a few hiring-process "principles" that have for far too long gone unquestioned and uncriticized.

One is nepotism. I get accused of this from time to time in the blogosphere, where some folks seem to assume that I "used" my rich connections in corporate America to land a job in finance. This was at a time just after the mortgage crisis and the ensuing recession, when getting a job in finance wasn't easy to do. Maybe the assumption is that I used family "connections" to get such a job. Well, my father worked for a packaging firm, my mother as an auditor, one grandfather was a dentist, the other was a veteran and small-business owner in Buffalo. So no, I didn't have a lot of strings to pull in 2010.

But I'll tell you this: if I had had the strings to pull, I would have pulled them all day and all night. My advice to anybody who has friends, relations, contacts of any shape or size in an industry or company you're interested in: wake the hell up and call them! There is nothing wrong about asking people you know for information, for a connection, even for help when it comes to getting a job—not so long as you're prepared to return the courtesy in some way, especially by lending a hand to another job seeker later on.

That's especially the case in an era when the job market is particularly competitive, as it was for me in 2010 when the economy was just emerging from a global financial crisis. The aftermath of the COVID-19 pandemic, which by April 2020 had left 14.8 percent of the working population in the United States unemployed,[1] is likely to see similarly high levels of competition for professional jobs.

The second unquestioned, uncriticized principle I'd like to question and criticize is the notion of "preparing for the interview." Yes, if you are granted a job interview, you should definitely be prepared with knowledge, with points you want to make, with precise and targeted questions. That's just for openers. During that interview, you will need an all-out strategy to sell yourself not just verbally but nonverbally as well, as I will make clear in the next chapter. But the fallacy about "preparing for the interview" is ass-backward. You should have prepared for the interview before you ever applied for the job.

In fact, why on earth would you even apply to companies you don't know enough about that you have to worry later about "studying up" before an interview? Reverse engineer that process from the start and apply only to companies that you do know well because you have already researched them. In doing that research, you have narrowed down your list to those companies that excite you, that produce products you want to be aligned with, that have a mission that makes you feel good, that have a company name you would be proud to tell people you work for. The kind of study that you would do for the interview is the kind of study you should be doing before applying for the job. Rather than spray and pray, flip the funnel upside down and spend your time on a smaller group of companies that really excite you.

One reason for this, as I will point out shortly, is that the corporate hiring process is geared to eliminate a full 90 percent of applicants right off the bat. Gone. Out the window. Good-freaking-bye to hours of application time and submission. This chapter shows you how to strategize to get to that interview—to get past the machines to the humans who will make the decisions. If you are waiting for an interview before studying up on a company, this is a lost cause.

The third principle about the hiring process I'd like to shoot down is the notion that the only job openings are those posted and that an applicant must answer *all* its requirements before applying. Simply not true. In fact, I did not meet all of the requirements listed in the job description for any job I have ever held. And neither did anybody else. I know because I asked all of them on day one of their new job. Every promotion I got I knew I had before the job was posted. In a word, job openings work a little like the housing market; real estate brokers love to show you the house that's going on sale before it hits the market.

What this means is that you can put yourself into a job via direct contact even if it is not officially "on the market." Some of the most exciting jobs may hover for a while during that "premarket" period.

Choosing the Companies You Will Pursue

First, however, you've got to determine which jobs to apply for. Since you know what kind of work you want to do and have an idea of which industries you'd like to work in, that determination should begin with figuring out which companies you would like to do the work for. Prepare yourself for a time-consuming commitment to internet surfing, but make it *targeted* surfing. Again, start with understanding yourself, your personality, the ways you create, solve problems, and handle conflict. I would highly recommend understanding your Enneagram[2] number or your personality type. Once you have mastered a profile of yourself, align your profession to that.

Then move on to your personal preferences: What are some companies you like? Maybe it's the company that makes the shoes, shades, bags, watch, car, coffee, beer, décor, art, wine, jewelry, or accessories you rock. Maybe it's a company that runs those brilliant, always funny commercials you see on YouTube, Instagram, TikTok, or TV. Or maybe it's the company that produces those commercials. Or perhaps it's the agency, brand, label, or team that represents a favorite celebrity, athlete, or musician. The examples are endless, but the heart of the matter is to get back to reframing yourself and creating a professional life that aligns with that person. Maybe there's a company you have your eye on in the place you decided you'd like to live; you're intrigued by its flat, organic structure. Another company, classically hierarchical, nevertheless seems to have a bang-up product development story. You're interested. It's a lot easier to see your future when you are paying close attention to what you naturally gravitate toward.

Next, look for the industries and the companies within them that are thriving. Even during the pandemic, there were thrivers: Amazon, Netflix, and Zoom, of course, but also consumer discretionary companies like those producing cleaning materials, as people staying at home full time went crazy keeping everything spotless and germ free. Sales of Pelotons soared, and they pretty much made their way to becoming the new normal for exercise. So did sales of personal safety products, online education courses, and houseplants! Delivery services of course flourished—especially Instacart, Uber Eats, Grubhub, and Post-mates in my house. Postpandemic, the list will only grow, but it will also change.

Make your lists, then do the kind of research people used to tell you to do before a job interview. Any company of interest, any company that you think may be a prospective employer, should be analyzed from top to bottom. If the company is publicly traded, investor.gov will show you its publicly published financials for free. You want to check out the company's 10-Q (quarterly reports) and 10-K (annual reports) and to understand the top- and bottom-line growth over time, how the company spends, and its management guidance. Those are the core available representations of a company's "behavior"—of how it functions and how well. And it's essential for deciding whether this is a company you think you might want to work for even for just a few years. Just identifying which companies have revenue growth in a particular year or economic cycle, regardless of profit, is an indication that those companies are well positioned for the future and that hiring is likely on the way.

But those are not the only standards on which to judge a company. Think also about how, in a sense, you will be *living in* the company that hires you, and make sure to research what that might be like. Start by talking to current employees at the company you're interested in—particularly people in entry-level roles. The reason? They are often much easier to access, more willing to talk, and can provide a bottom-up perspective on the company and its culture—the very sort of "stuff" you cannot get by checking out a website or mission statement. In fact, taking a current employee out for coffee just may offer the best ROI in the job market.

So, by all means, deconstruct the standard way of looking at companies and challenge its assumptions and contradictions. Prepare for your job-seeking campaign by allowing yourself to get excited about some companies you think you would enjoy working for to the mutual profit of both the company and you!

It's a great first step, and, subconsciously, it is the first step of the interview preparation process.

Then, trust me: forget almost everything you thought you knew about the hiring process.

Hiring: Another Design in the Blueprint

Today's corporate hiring process is part of the same blueprint handed down to you at birth, the one that got you the job you're now trying to get out of. It's broken, just like many of our careers, companies, titles, and compensation standards. This time, however, before putting it to work to get you the restart you want, you'll at least enter the process with your eyes wide open. Open them, for example, to the reality that the standard hiring process seduces us with inflated titles and lavish job descriptions meant to impress and, in a sense, to distract and very nearly anesthetize us.

Vice president of operations overseeing day-to-day activities across different departments responsible for growth! Strategy officer responsible for developing, communicating, and executing corporate strategic initiatives! Vice president for marketing in charge of facilitating growth and driving sales! These imposing titles and responsibilities demand respect; they almost compel admiration. They are big titles projecting the need for an exorbitant amount of required experiences and acquired skills, and almost no single individual could possibly have all the listed "job requirements." Well, at least the requirements they post online.

I'll say something else about these corporate titles. I remember swelling with pride when I got my first title, assistant vice president, AVP! Until I realized that virtually everybody around me was an AVP or higher. So I yearned to become a VP and really stand out. Well, when I got there, I again realized I was part of a crowd. By the time the bank made me a senior corporate banker (not quite a senior vice president), I had figured out that that title, like all the other titles I had either had or could strive for, was absolutely empty. These titles don't really mean a thing. They just feed your ego, and for that reason, they're another tool the company can use to engage your enthusiasm and loyalty at almost no cost. I think they're bullshit, and human resources executives know it, but they advertise them like crazy all over the place. Their goal is to cast as wide a net as possible to ensure that they can choose from the biggest possible pool of candidates. Titles are just part of the allure.

For those of us applying for the job with the alluring title, however, that means that we start out the job search deflated, knowing that our qualifications are a bit short of the mark. (And if we do land a job, we feel we've been given a gift for which we are not just grateful but also downright honored.) Among the HR experts posting the job, however, there is a formidable strategy at work behind the inflated titles and the intimidating job descriptions—a reason that job applicants feel humbled by them. To understand the strategy, put yourself in the place of the companies doing the hiring. Seen through their eyes, the whole process is a somewhat scary liability threat. Personnel is one of the most important variables in any organization. It can cost tens of thousands of dollars to cull the surging onrush of applications that pour into a company's computers, then to select, hire, pay, extend benefits to, and take a chance on an individual based solely on two pieces of paper and, most likely, under two hours of face-to-face interviewing. People spend more time than that before they accept a first date! This is why companies hire HR recruiters, consultants, and tech experts to design a process and algorithms that will filter out what ends up being about 90 percent of the applications, résumés, emails, social media messages, referrals, and the like that pour into their computers in response to a single job announcement.

The process is set up for you to fail. It is aimed at efficiency. The odds are simply stacked against you, especially in an economic era when you are up against not only the usual just-out-of-school competitors but also students dealing with debt burdens and looking hard to step up. Plus people as unhappy in their current job as you are in yours. Plus those shaken by COVID-19. Now these folks are looking to restart *their* careers. Simply put, we're in a moment when the number of applicants looking for work is at an all-time high, and even a surging economy might not be able to fit them all in. Count on lots of competition.

And accept the reality that overstated job descriptions are a mirage of perfection. Best position and place to be, and wow! You should be flattered that you've even been considered to interview for a job you're not even remotely qualified for. All part of the bullshit you will have to navigate your way through. The only way to beat the numbers game the HR algorithms put you through is to rethink the hiring process so you can reverse engineer it to your advantage. To do that, you need to assume the company's point of view and devise a strategy that shows the company that *hiring you will reduce the liability threat built into its hiring process.* I'll say that again another way: show the company's HR team and hiring managers, the people actually in need of someone to do the job in question, that you'll do said job competently, thereby reducing their overall hiring risk and thus checking the "system" box, and you are as good as hired. I personally executed this strategy eight times in my almost ten years of working in the "system."

How do you do it? Start by picturing the typical HR decision maker. Let's call him Tim. He is tasked with finding precisely the right individual for the high-level position you're applying for. The company, the hiring manager offering the position, the HR team, and Tim wrote the job posting, carefully designed the questions you answered in the online questionnaire, came up with the list of qualifications and range of experience needed, and are aware that there is probably no single human being who possesses all the qualifications or the full range of experience. Tim, the decision maker, has also read a lot of résumés and cover letters in his career, has conducted more interviews than he can count, and knows how to interpret what he reads and hears. Your aim is to get savvy, successful, seen-every-trick-in-the-book Tim to read your entire application, every word of your cover letter, and all of your résumé so that he is impressed enough to look for you in other media formats and to invite you for an interview. To do that, you will, in each of those formats in which you connect with him, present yourself as the individual who for the lowest cost and with the least "trouble" will provide the company the strengths it seeks. In a nutshell, find ways to make Tim's job move more efficiently and smoothly by showing him how hiring you will reduce his decision-making risk.

The process you must complete for Tim is the same process the artificial intelligence technology now uses to search and scan all résumés that mirror the posted job description. The whole reason companies pay big bucks for this AI function is that it is aimed at kicking out the majority of applicants. Only those applications that are a perfect match in terms of experience required and skills needed survive this AI run, and only those surviving applicants who are still interested and still available get invited to meet in person. The vast majority of applications, including yours and mine, are tossed.

Conclusion? You have got to go the direct route, outthinking the system and beating it before it beats you.

In fact, the direct route will also reduce your own turnover risk. Throwing as many applications as possible against the corporate wall just multiplies your chances of getting no response whatsoever. One sharply reasoned attempt aimed precisely at Tim's liability risk has a better chance of a response.

What will show that to Tim?

Of course, every job is different, and every company has its own ways of doing things. But HR has its own concerns and priorities, and to the extent that you can show Tim how hiring you will cool those concerns and advance his priorities, the better your chances of at least getting his attention so that you can possibly persuade him. Even the monstrosity of Amazon has a system in which a referral from a highly regarded employee sends your application right to the top. Good luck trying to submit an application blind without that kind of referral. Let me put it in my Buffalo unprofessional tone: if you throw shit at the wall hoping something sticks, I promise you'll get shit results!

For example, the chances are good that Tim and the hiring manager would like to hire somebody who has the skill set, the experience, the energy, and the temperament to be able to step into the job this morning, quickly master procedures unique to the company, and by the end of the day be in charge. Tim wants to be able to rely on the new hire's attention to the well-being of all employees and to his or her commitment to diversity and inclusion. And of course he wants to retain top talent. Tim would be pleased to know that the job candidate (you, for example) has the perception and discernment to realize quickly what the top priorities of the position are and to design plans for all of them. In addition, Tim knows all too well that technological change and the spread of artificial intelligence may well affect all aspects of the company and its industry, and he wants someone who is both equipped to understand such changes and flexible enough to implement them successfully. Finally, he wants someone who can train their own successor as they move up from or out of the position.

Find ways to show Tim and the hiring manager you would end up reporting to that you fit the profile of an individual who can answer all those concerns, and you'll lower the temperature of their liability worries.

Where should this strategy of reducing liability threat start? Right at the beginning of the process, with the creation of your brand.

Defining Your Brand

When I was starting out in my career, I thought of my brand as the characteristics that would tell people how to think about me. I saw it really as "showing" how I *wanted* to be perceived.

Here's a tip: that doesn't work. It is a "strategy" with absolutely no longevity. Why not? Because nothing about such a brand will correlate with who you really are or the job you can and want to do.

Instead, find what differentiates you, your superpowers. We all have them! I mentioned back in chapter three that when I met the guys I was up against on *The Bachelorette*, I realized that while I lacked their obvious strengths, I had one they seemed to lack: I could "read the room." I had an intuitive ability to quickly grasp what people in a group were feeling and thinking—an important strength in relationship banking and, as it turned out, in the world of reality TV. So of course everybody applying for a particular position is going to claim expertise in the basic qualifications set forth in the job posting. Instead of that, think hard about the singular, specific, detailed assets of personal strength and professional capability over and above what it says in the posting. Which assets will add value to your performance? That's the brand you want printed on the minds of those who are doing the hiring.

Then, own your brand. Make everything else correlate with it: your résumé, your cover letter, and, of course, everything that you do on social media—your likes, comments, searches, all of it. That latter correlation is particularly important because the "wrong" social media representation can kill a brand in no time at all, as I'm pretty sure I don't have to tell you. Every week seems to bring a new example of the latest celebrity, business leader, or politician losing his or her reputation when tweets from long ago are suddenly uncovered and publicized.

This isn't just about making sure you haven't done anything offensive; it's also about keeping attuned to who you are today.

People change, and people learn. The clicks, likes, and comments that recorded who you were five years ago or more might not be in tune with who you are today. Human beings can transform themselves from foolish and irresponsible blockheads into responsible grown-ups, so you want to be sure that what reflects back on you as a person and as a professional today is up to date and in sync with the person you're projecting to the world. We live in a digital world, and so does your past. Make it a habit to review the clicks, likes, retweets, and comments that "reflect" you online, and revise or annul as needed. You know how to do it: anywhere you have a profile in social media, click on settings, take time to review *everything*, and make sure it matches today's you. If it doesn't, erase!

The Résumé/Cover Letter

I know: it's totally crazy to try reducing your life's work and your worth as a job candidate onto a single piece of paper (or a few pieces of paper anyway) in a résumé and cover letter. And there's no question that, thanks again to online features and social media, the nature of the résumé is changing drastically, even as I write this.

But whatever form the résumé and cover letter eventually take, it will still constitute a core statement of who you are as a person and as a candidate for the job in question. It's in the (typically) one-page résumé that you define and describe your brand in a tightly written, action-packed, limited number of words: a paragraph telling who you are and what you bring to the organization, buttressed by a bulleted list of the relevant facts that bring that description to life. You couch this impressive branding statement in a cover letter that explains briskly but potently why you believe you should be hired for the job that has been posted.

These messages make the résumé/cover letter an important document, and it needs to *look* it. It isn't just the words you use but also the appearance it bears; the setup and positioning of the information, the fonts you choose, the design, the tone you strike, and for in-person interviews even the quality of the paper on which it's printed. All of this will impact the reader.

One of my first "side hustles" after graduating from SUNY Geneseo was to create, along with my good friend Hawk, a company we called ResReview—an online, one-on-one, résumé and cover letter "service company." We charged from $50 to $250 and covered all professions. The majority of our clients were friends and, thanks to referrals, the friends of friends. My major takeaway from that experience is that, where the most important professional document in any career is concerned, fewer than 5 percent of people have any idea what they're doing. Doctors, lawyers, accountants, physical therapists, teachers, business development officers—none of them did an even halfway presentable job. You would think that people who spent years in postgraduate professional schools, paying out uber amounts of money doing it, would apply some of the same energy to the document that would help them accomplish what they were working for. That some of them wrote impressive, distinctive PhD theses but couldn't write a résumé mystifies me to this day.

Why does it matter so much? Because of the purpose. These two documents encapsulate who you are, list every damn bit of work you have done to get there, and tell the reader why you should get this job. Keep in mind that they will be Tim's first "look" at you—the first impression you make on the hiring manager and the HR group, your first chance to achieve the absolutely crucial goal of catching their attention and interest. Again, tailor what you say to their needs—and specifically to the precise verbiage of the posted job description—and offer examples of accomplishments that speak to those needs. As best you can, keeping in mind the goal of differentiating yourself as the candidate who can reduce Tim's risk of liability, make it a document that will inspire the people doing the hiring to go on to all the succeeding media formats in which you and they will "meet"—most of which will be online.

The Internet and Social Media

Change is the only constant in our world, and that goes for the hiring process too. At some point in the near future, I suspect that résumés and cover letters will become obsolete; until then, you have to nail yours.

Still, the time to get onto what's next is now. Every reader of this book needs to own the URL of his or her own name and to have a proprietary website. My website is JasonTartick.com, and you can email me at media@JasonTartick.com. Couldn't be simpler, and it will differentiate those dragging to get with the times. The website is your portfolio; it shows who you are and the work you've done. It establishes the credibility of the work you *will* do. Think of it as your résumé on steroids; it expands on your brand in a way that is comfortable for people to browse. And it is not hard or complex to build; there is plenty of help out there for getting the website you want. GoDaddy, Wix, Network Solutions, Squarespace, and many more. The more creative among us (those who like to play around with design features) may be satisfied with a free website builder. But even at a price, this is a business expense you can't afford *not* to invest in. Not to mention that there are so many resources for finding web designers at an affordable price. I have used upwork.com, hired.com, and github.com. And there are many more to be found in a simple Google search.

Use your website's About section to tell your story. Show your work by posting examples of what you've done and by telling what you have accomplished or achieved. Offer references, testimonials, work, and education history. Urge people to email you. Include your online résumé and cover letter. Take a stab at blogging as a forum for talking about your expertise, abilities, and achievements and for suggesting what you're ready to do next.

Doing this will increase your overall SEO—search engine optimization. It is *your* website; you are its executive editor, and you can put there whatever you think is relevant to what you're hoping to achieve next.

You can also set up tracking pixels on your site so that you can monitor who is visiting the site and can follow such specifics as when and for how long. These kinds of data can lead you to qualified companies and the individuals in them doing research on you.

If you don't yet have a LinkedIn profile, start creating one now.

Yet that's just the beginning of the online presence you need to create and maintain regularly. Every reader of this book also needs to have almost every form of social media there is: LinkedIn, Facebook, Twitter, Instagram, TikTok, Clubhouse, Pinterest, You-Tube, and whatever comes next. You don't need to be active on all of them; on the contrary, suit the forum or forums to the brand you are trying to broadcast.

The one must-have social media platform for your restart is LinkedIn. In fact, make yourself a LinkedIn warrior! It is a must not just because it is pretty much the granddaddy of business sites and the place where professionals really do gather, but mostly because of its power as a job-finding platform. With more than seven hundred million members in two hundred countries, it is unsurpassed at linking open jobs to candidates. Hubspot has claimed that LinkedIn is "227 percent more effective at generating leads than Facebook and Twitter" together.

There's more. An outfit called Skrapp offers a way to find the email addresses of people you want to connect with in LinkedIn. It's completely legal and aboveboard, and it's the perfect way to introduce yourself to the potential leads you identify on the site. It may make sense to connect with those HR recruiters and hiring managers directly via an email or LinkedIn direct message. Here's the link: https://skrapp.io/tutorials/linkedin-email-finder-profile. It is another useful way to beat the "standard" system, the one that is designed to weed out most job applicants.

Again, LinkedIn is a necessity. If you don't yet have a LinkedIn profile, start creating one now. You'll need a clean, crisp headshot and a tone similar to that of your résumé and cover letter. This is a key forum for demonstrating you, your brand, and your added value! The faster you become a LinkedIn warrior, the sooner you will find your dream job at the perfect company for you.

Upending Your "Getting Hired" Process

Defining your brand, committing it to "paper" and to a website, and mastering the social media scene all constitute essential preparation for the actual process of submitting job applications. The first step in that process will remind you of the police investigations on those *CSI* or cop shows we've all been watching on TV since we were kids. Remember? After the crime has occurred, the investigators gather all the leads they can. They're not sure of the meaning of any of the leads at first, so they just keep collecting any and all information they can find. The more information they have, the better.

Same with getting the job that will be your restart. The aim is to get through to the decision maker, the individual who will actually do the hiring for the particular job you're after. Separating you from that individual is a set of formalities, many of them required by law. Your aim as a job seeker will be to try to get in front of that process. The first step is to gather and organize all the information you can about the companies you want to work for, the job you're seeking, the pay being offered, the competencies required, and anything and everything else.

Start with the companies. Apart from liking or being intrigued by a set of potential employers, which ones align with your determinants of career success? Will your skill set be used to the full? Will compensation or mobility be a problem? Is this a company that will allay any fears you may have? Can it play into your passion and even kick it up a notch? Do the companies you're exploring support local, regional, or national not-for-profits that align with your values? Make a list of the companies that pass the test, those you would be glad and even proud to work for. Then, rank the companies in order of preference: the top three, top five, top ten, or whatever works for you. This is your prospect list, which will inevitably lead to your restart. This list should live in your notes, email, on your watch—it needs to be always accessible. Make everyone you know, as well as everyone you meet, aware of where you want to work and why. Be absolutely clear about exactly where you want your next step to be and then communicate that message precisely to anyone and everyone. You will never manifest your next step without that clarity and without communicating it widely. In fact, make it a damn habit to broadcast the message to anyone who will listen: friends, family, former classmates, recruiters, even the barista at Starbucks—anyone!

Next, within that batch of companies, identify what you want out of a job there in terms of compensation, title, position, and responsibilities. Also rank the top three or top five or top ten positions you want, the responsibilities you seek, and the compensation packages you will ask for.

In my case, I ranked my top twenty across all of those measures.

Yes, it was a lot of work. But it became the basis for my search for what I call a "toasty takedown"—someone, anyone, who had some sort of connection to each of the companies on my list. No matter how tenuous, some form of connection is better than making a cold call on your own. Finding such connections is fairly easy in the days of emails and social media.

I also ranked the "power" of each connection in terms of what the individual could bring to my job search: cool, tepid, warm, hot, or toasted. Did the individual have a connection with a hiring manager (toasted), or past experience with the company (warm), or a cousin in the company's HR department (hot), or an ex-girlfriend in finance (cool: it had been an unpleasant breakup)? I scrolled through my contacts and my emails going back years to find these connections and was only mildly surprised at the number that popped up. You really do meet an awful lot of people as you grow up, go to school, attend college, and go to work. There's treasure in tracking them down for a task like this one. It is another reason why it's important to have social media: namely, immediate access to all your contacts. If you follow someone on one social media forum, you should follow that person on all forums. Of course, not all are meant for professional networking, but carefully curating this natural network is incredibly important in your journey.

Yes, ranking my connections was also a lot of work. But the aim was to transform a system built to work against me into a mechanism that could work *for* me. Otherwise, I believed, I would just be sending résumé after résumé to some huge, blank fortress built to work against me. If that isn't throwing shit at the wall, I don't know what is.

I did indeed reach out to every single contact on my list. And the contact I found in the end was an executive in one of my top three companies. The connection? The man had coached junior varsity hockey with my father.

This was not a guy who had ever coached *me*; I got lucky and made the varsity team as a freshman, only to ride the pine most of the year. But I digress. In going through all my social media, I identified that the guy had coached alongside my father, and when my father confirmed the connection, I reached out to him in what I worked hard to make a strong and strategic introductory email.

He responded by phoning me. I was ready with a two-minute speech aimed at introducing myself further and telling him what I was after. He was actually impressed! He remembered my dad with great affection, was thrilled that I wanted to come work for the company he had dedicated his entire career to, and proceeded to put the right word in the right ear. I got the job, a 60 percent raise, and, when I was lured back to the bank nine months later, managed another raise of more than 50 percent. So the bottom line of my admittedly laborious process to find the right connection in the right place for the right move had an enormous impact on my career overall. I benefit from it to this day.

By the way, I found the connection on LinkedIn—just by searching executives in companies within a hundred-mile radius and entering the company name. Another plus for this formidable site.

I was twenty-four when I took that job. Everybody around me was in their midthirties or forties. I had none of the experience the job posting claimed was "essential." Zero! But I found a way in, and once in, I offered experience measured in other ways: not in time spent but in projects realized and, I think it is fair to say, in exhibiting enterprise and energy. Bottom line? You *can* get the job you want.

This suggests to me—and I hope to you—that the time so many of us spend looking online for vague "influencers" could be more profitably spent stalking companies we like. I don't mean the word in the sense of "creeping up on." Rather, I mean keeping track of everything the company is doing. If you like the way a company operates or love the products it makes, why not keep up with everything about it just in case you someday want to become a part of it? Here's a test for you: if your phone provides screen-time stats, start managing your screen time to the day, hour, and minute. That should help you invest your time where it needs to be: in you and this process. If your phone shows you're clocking more time tracking your team's line scores or checking your Twitter feed than on monitoring the companies you're interested in, flip that equation ASAP.

The bottom line of the standard hiring process, as noted, is that it is set up to cast as wide a net as possible, not to hunt for the white whale—the singular "prize." That makes it hard for any one individual to stand out. What I'm advocating is for you to find your way to upend the process to your advantage. Change the way you brand yourself. Use the information you gather about companies you like to identify the many pathways that can take you there.

Don't stop there. Use every tool at your disposal, many of which are close at hand. For example, get in touch with local business and civic leaders. Of necessity, they have their fingers on the pulse of the economy. They know its premier business organizations, and they are easy to connect with because connecting is their job. These individuals typically create associations by profession: a bankers' association, a retailers' association, lawyers' groups, accountants' groups, even elected officials' caucuses. Within and across groups, they share with one another what's going on; it's key to their success. Bankers serve the big businesses in an area and know which of their clients are thriving and hiring. Retailers have their finger on the pulse of what's selling and what's not. Lawyers are into everything and know all the main players.

Keep tabs also on what's going on in nearby universities and community colleges when it comes to job fairs and recruiting.

Check in with the nearest chapter of SHRM, the Society for Human Resource Management, the huge membership organization of HR managers. They are likely to work with most of the big businesses in the area.

Get to know every recruiter you can find, and identify any and all industry events in your area. Recruiters know which positions in which companies need to be filled, and decision makers routinely attend industry events.

And nobody is more attuned to what's going on than journalists. To find out what they know, you often need to tell them something *you* know that they don't. It is usually worth the swap.

All the Shit That's Fit to Stick

- ↯ Nepotism is good. If you have strings to pull, pull them! There's nothing wrong about asking people you know for information, for a connection, even for help when it comes to getting a job—as long as you're prepared to return the courtesy.

- ↯ Of course you need a job interview strategy. But you should begin to prepare for a job interview before you even apply for the job. The corporate hiring process is geared to eliminate a full 90 percent of applicants right off the bat, so you need a strategy to get past the gatekeepers at companies where you want to work. It begins with deep research into companies where you may want to apply.

- ↯ Obsessed with titles? They don't really mean a thing. They're another tool the company can use to engage your loyalty at almost no cost.

- ↯ Your brand is what differentiates you. It's your superpower. Own it. Be sure your résumé, cover letter, and all your social media are aligned with it. Your résumé and cover letter constitute a core statement of who you are as a person and as a candidate for the job in question. These documents should be aligned with the values of companies where you want to work. It's imperative that these documents be dynamic; tweak them to suit the company and position you are after.

- ↯ The one must-have social media platform for your restart is LinkedIn.

7

The Art of Getting Noticed

Repositioning How You Present Yourself

*O*f course, I think every chapter of this book is vitally important, but if there is one chapter among them all that has the
potential to create the most value for you, it is probably this one.
Grasp what you read here and execute what it puts forward, and
you are on your way to the restart you seek and a career that will
pay endless dividends.

It all comes down to selling.

I know: for some, the very word *selling* carries a negative con-
notation, as if there were something a bit greasy or even shameful
about it. To others, the idea of selling is intimidating: the necessity
to prepare for an interview or presentation by figuring out exactly
how you should dress, talk, act, communicate. It can all be mind
boggling, exhausting, and too much to deal with.

So let's get straight right from the get-go what we mean when
we talk about selling.

The fact is that every second of every day you are selling and being sold to. With what you wear, in every conversation, in every experience, you are putting forward who you are and are simultaneously receiving "sales presentations" from the people, places, and activities you deal with. In a grocery store, you are being "sold to" the moment you walk in the door, starting with whatever the social scientists and polling experts determined was the best kind of signage for getting your attention without annoying you. Ah ha! Aisle 3 is what they've convinced you that you want, and when you get there and start reviewing the various brands, you're being sold by the label, the colors, the special deal, the commercial you saw the other day. And you're "selling back" through the choices you make.

Of course the smartest of grocery stores put the essentials in the farthest corner possible from the entrance. You want your damn milk and eggs? Well, good luck passing the other thousand items on your way to that back corner of the store, then back again to checkout, without picking up anything else.

I think of training my two dogs as a selling process. I am selling when I ask one of them to sit; the dog is selling me by obeying, and the treat I offer seals the deal. That's a sale. The dog and I have provided each other value. It's a win-win transaction.

The same is true for my Seattle Hairgate—when my bosses at the bank "suggested" I change my hairstyle. They were selling me on a look that would represent *them* as they wanted to be represented; I sold that to them in return for knowing that in two more years at the bank I would have enough money saved up to get out.

This universal predisposition for selling—seemingly as natural as breathing—is something I believe we learn early in life, probably when we first start sharing toys and making friends. And it never stops. So, like it or not, aware of it or not, you are always selling, in the way you position yourself, the way you act, what you say, and what you don't say.

An interview I did with Chrishell Stause, the well-known actress who doubles as an agent on the TV series *Selling Sunset*, adds an interesting twist to selling with what you *don't* say. Although Chrishell is both an Emmy-nominated star and an agent at a premier real estate group, Oppenheim, she is also aware that she is sometimes "treated differently as a woman." In the high-powered Los Angeles real estate universe in which she operates, there are, she says, "some very rich men who like to think that they know it all." This is of course frustrating, but Stause's way of dealing with it is to "use it to my advantage." She just stays "two steps ahead of them," lets them show off, and reminds herself that although she has to put up with this silliness, she doesn't have to "let that kind of energy affect my day."

It's unlikely that the world of real estate or the world in general will ever be totally rid of dumbasses who need to show off. So do as Chrishell does: let them think it was all their brilliant idea. And get the thing sold!

What is essential for your restart is to remember that what you are selling now is your new understanding of who you are and of what constitutes success in your eyes. Forget the interview "tips" you read in the latest business magazine article. Forget the business influencers screaming so loud that they are spitting, or the ones dropping "fuck" every other word to sound relatable (a selling tactic). Forget the jargon you use in corporate meetings or emails so you can impress the hiring manager. Stop curating conversations so you can give back to the person you're talking to the exact same thing he just said to you but in different words. You got off that train when you picked up this book. What this chapter helps you sell is everything you learned in the hard work of self-examination and of probing your priorities. That work showed you who you are. And who you are is precisely what you're selling today. This chapter shows you how to position, project, and promote that person both in words and without them. It's all about how to shape and deliver your best value so that you can land the restart you want and negotiate successfully for the terms you seek. Make it your textbook on getting noticed the way you want to be noticed.

Selling 101: The First Impression

You know the line: you never get a second chance to make a first impression. Here's another: you only get seconds to make the first impression to begin with. And here's my take: making the right first impression is absolutely imperative.

Why? Like it or not, fair or not, this is the presentation you deliver that establishes how you and your intent are recognized, judged, and distinguished from everybody else. It establishes how you are perceived. And you can't take it back. There is no way to undo a so-so first impression, to modify it after the fact, to edit it with a follow-up email or phone conversation. It's one and done: you had your shot, you blew it, you're out of here.

In fact, it has been shown that it takes eight noticeably impressive actions to recoup a bad first impression.[1] Eight positive, observable, successful undertakings—an achievement or execution or implementation or fulfillment due solely to you, to your ability, to your performance. That's what it takes to wipe away the ill effects of a bad or mediocre or totally shit first impression. How much work typically goes into achieving eight successes? What would it feel like to see them rendered meaningless in a few seconds?

So the absolutely last thing you want to have happen when you are aiming for your restart and presenting yourself in a wholly new way is to blow the first impression. There's no margin for error here; when you're putting this much of your life, your career, your vision of success on the line, you need to make the right first impression.

Start by understanding that there are two elements of market-ing that are at work in any self-presentation: the nonverbal and the verbal. That is, communication without using words or speech, and communication *through* words and speech. Both types of communication are potent marketing mechanisms and will serve as essential sales tools.

Nonverbals are like the lights and camera of a first impression; what you say and how you say it are the action. Nonverbals estab-lish an atmosphere and project an image that you hope is appeal-ing and confident; verbals disclose what you're aiming for. Clearly, getting a first impression right (and remember, you only have one shot at it) means being able to control every single detail of the first impression you make. That requires planning that covers ev-ery eventuality the first meeting could possibly present you with. "Every single detail" of course means both the nonverbals and the verbals. To control your nonverbals, you'll need to tune in to the body language of others and at the same time project in your body language the impression you want to get across. Controlling your verbals means writing your own opinions, thoughts, and ideas ahead of time and reviewing what you've written so well that it's all at the tip of your tongue when you need it. Easy and fluid. It's your safety net; if you get backed into a corner, the verbals that will get you out of the corner are right there, as safe in your head as if they were in your pocket. Reach for them, pull them out, and you're good. In my view, that means preparing a minimum of five "power lines," as I call them, for any and every situation you're about to enter—a meeting, a sales opportunity, a job interview for sure. Knowing you have those power lines under control offers a foundation of confidence that keeps you in charge of your overall first-impression "performance."

I'll have more to say about power lines later on, but let me begin by telling you how, once I had made the decision to go all in on *The Bachelorette*, I began planning my first impression as a "suitor":

the act of emerging from the limo. I meant it as a way of standing apart from the other contestants and of proclaiming what I perceived as my unique value right from the get-go. And I figured the only way to do that was to think through every single detail.

It began in the hotel where the contestants are housed for about a week before the show begins. You're in a room without a phone or internet. You cannot leave, and you never know when one or more of the producers is going to knock on the door, come in, and shoot the shit, which they did at least twice a day. It was clear they wanted to get to know each one of us. I felt as though they were mentally taking notes about whether our rooms were neat and clean, if we were funny, if we were sharp, if we were careless, cocky, or arrogant, if we qualified as a good guy, a great guy, a douchebag, or a total loser. I treated it as another interview; every discussion with a producer was a selling session. I was selling to them, and they were selling to me.

I saw this as a challenge to make a great first impression on the producers. To me, each of them was "the boss," and in my opinion, if one or all of them didn't like me, I could get dropped from the show before it ever started. So, every time there was a knock on the door, I went into first-impression delivery mode as soon as the guy or gal entered the room, tried to stand out from the other contestants, and gave him or her what I believed was my best self. I began by proactively pitching them differentiating ideas for coming out of the limo.

I made it clear that I didn't want to be a guy exiting the limo in a chicken costume or on a horse or in any way visibly trying to make a rousing, electrifying first impression on Becca Kufrin, our Bachelorette. Instead, I told the producers, "I am going to be who I am, with a simple entrance that both shows and tells Becca the particular message I bring." I told them that I was confident that I knew myself, understood who I am, and would absolutely stay within the confines throughout the show. While I couldn't control all that much of anything at this point in the journey (couldn't even have my phone!), I always remembered that "I can control what I am and what I do."

I laid it out for them precisely, leveraging all the principles about self-selling and about shaping and delivering value that are at the heart of this chapter. In a very real sense, I was creating my first impression on the producers—I guess you could say on the bosses—by *describing* how I would create my first impression.

First step: a custom-made blue suit and shirt designed to be subtle and professional but to emit a tone of blue that would stand out and pop from the navy blue of the suit; at the very least, it would speak to my sense of self. I would also bring her a meaningful gift that symbolized the journey ahead, my message, and our first encounter. The gift was champagne, which I would serve in two champagne flutes engraved with my family's customary toast, which wishes for "health, wealth, love, happiness—and all the time in the world to enjoy!" Gift and toast both answered to what I genuinely value highly: family and friends. And if that message didn't resonate with Becca, then nothing I could say or do would. So much for nonverbal.

For verbal, I recited for the producers the introduction I had prepared for when I stepped out of the limo. It went something like this: "Hi, Becca, my name is Jason, and I am from Buffalo, New York. Something you don't know about me that I want you to know is that my parents have been together for thirty-five years, and I have personally witnessed their love for each other grow every day. One of the best parts of their relationship is that they are best friends. I don't know about you, but my best friends and I back home all meet with handshakes. You and I need to start somewhere. . . ." I would extend my hand. "So give me a bop-bop and a 'hell, yeah!'" Simple, a bit goofy, but to the point, and me.

The producers' reaction? "Perfect," they said. "This all works." Which totally shocked me. I was waiting for the pitch to wear a chicken or cupcake costume and was ready with the outrageous counter. Nope, they said, "Perfect! Go for it!"

It turned out that most of the other contestants had no plan at all.

My weird, bizarre takeaway from this approval of my plan for walking out of a damn limo on a national stage to make a first impression was confirmation of what I totally believe in: that you need to differentiate yourself, that you can only do it by aligning with who you really are, and that the way to do it is to control everything in life that you possibly can through productive planning. In fact, when it was my turn to emerge from the limo, I followed this script to the letter. I am sure you'll be surprised to hear that it took about one second of airtime. Why? I believe that was because it wasn't an outrageous stunt to drive attention or ratings. It was just me! Maybe a bit boring, but I wasn't looking for screen time, I was looking to make an authentic impression. The rest is *Bachelorette* history and the beginning of my personal restart.

Silent Selling: Making Your Nonverbal Presentation Work for You

All our "communications," verbal and nonverbal, have an impact on others' perceptions. Whatever you may intend to say aloud during your verbal communication, all sorts of unspoken "statements" will also shape the presentation you're making and the impression you leave. Did you arrive on time? Did you shave this morning? What are you wearing? Did you put on perfume or cologne? Do you smell like the breakfast you made? These speak for you as loudly as the words you utter and the fluency with which you talk.

The most outrageous but also the best example of nonverbal communication I've ever come across is the whole red-carpet phenomenon. In my view, the red carpet is the quintessence of nonverbal communication. Hang with me for a second and let me explain.

The simple act of a celebrity walking down the red carpet is an event to which an army of skilled professionals will typically devote months of work. The reason? That moment on the red carpet—celebrity poised, smile fixed, minimal movements, typically not a word spoken, cameras clicking incessantly—is worth a fortune, not just to the celebrity but also to the army of professionals involved in that selling process. That army includes a stylist, a wardrobe guru, hairdresser, makeup artist, shoe specialist, jewelry selector, accessories expert, assigned escort, posture instructor, acting coach who shows the celebrity how to stand and what vibe to project, publicists, and of course the celebrity's manager who has worked like hell organizing, negotiating, and applying all possible pressure to get the right time slot (the later in the evening one walks, the greater the notoriety) and to make certain the cameras capture just the right "look." All for these few seconds his or her "star" will stand on the red carpet.

All of these people—plus their assistants and gofers and aides—do all of this for months on end for a photograph that will potentially appear once in a magazine. Why? Because when the photograph is spotted by someone standing in the checkout line at the grocery store, someone scrolling on social media, or someone in the dentist's waiting room, that can add up to a photo that has been spotted by tens of millions of people. For the army, as well as for the celebrity, that is a phenomenal marketing impact. Any number of people among those tens of millions may want to buy the same shoes or gown or jewelry the celebrity wore in the photo, or to know the products used by the glam expert doing the makeup on that A-list celebrity, or to track down the accessories associated with that photo of the celebrity, thus bringing more business to the members of the army along with yet more interest in the celebrity.

That is the potential impact of one damn photo, a nonverbal presentation: an exponential multiplication of the impact you make.

And nonverbal is not just the way you look. It is also the way your body is speaking—that is, what your body language is saying.

Amy Cuddy, known for one of the most popular TED talks of all time—"Your Body Language May Shape Who You Are"—stands strongly behind the idea that "power posing" can increase confidence and the likelihood of success.

To me, the best example of what I mean is found in poker, a game I love. The facedown cards in poker represent information, and the essence of the game is always to get more information, especially more than you give away. Just as in life, the more information you have acquired, the better you can project outcome and the easier the decision-making process becomes. Body language is the means of doing both. You're getting information out of the other players while trying to keep them from getting information out of you. A good poker player is constantly watching the body language of the other players to gain all the information he or she can soak up, while at the same time consciously projecting his or her own body language in ways that conceal their own information.

It happens in everything the players do: the way they touch their cards, play with their chips, and whether they are thrust forward or leaning back in their seats. They are selling as hard as they can to get more information and at the same time providing as little information as possible so as to raise their chances of making the decisions that inevitably lead to winning. All through probability and assessing the nonverbals.

I would notice somebody's neck pulsing and would take away from that the information that the player was nervous or excited. Maybe a player would raise his hands to his face, indicating to me a kind of edginess. Or suddenly a player might speak in a sort of aggressive tone. I took that to mean the player thought he had a soft hand but was attempting to show strength. I worked to understand these as signals, but they also reminded me to keep a "poker face" and not give anything away through my own nonverbal body language.

I may have had an advantage in my reading of other people's body language thanks to a "seminar" on body-language consulting when I worked for the bank. I found it interesting and useful.

I remember learning that a palm-up handshake meant that the person was open to you, while a palm-down handshake was a statement of power, a statement that he or she was superior to you. The instructor suggested that if the boss were to shake your hand with the palm down, the thing to do was to hold the hand briefly, then flip the handshake 90 degrees. Accept the power statement, then rotate it to neutral to show your confidence.

I also learned that a person holding his or her arms closed across the chest is not, as most of us suppose, feeling unwelcome in the conversation. On the contrary, the gesture is actually a sign of inner comfort and support. People who lean back when they are seated have confidence in the conversation. If they lean forward, it indicates they are intrigued and actively involved in what's being said. I also learned that people who keep looking at or playing with their watch, or who continually remove lint from their clothing, or who are otherwise jittery are probably irritated and annoyed by the way the conversation is going. Take whatever action you think wise.

Hollywood and poker represent two different "trades" and two different ways that nonverbals play out. But awareness of the nonverbals, both those you're communicating with and those you're "reading," is an essential that applies not just to every line of work but to everything you do. Always read the body language of the people you're with: how someone makes eye contact, what a person is wearing, even how a person smells. What is the message in how this guy keeps twirling his Montblanc pen—or in the fact that he even has a Montblanc? What is the message in the fixed smile on the face of that person asking me questions? What are the strengths these people are trying to show me? What are the weaknesses I perceive in them?

And how do I position myself so that they see what I want them to see? How do I take control of the way I move my hands, what I'm wearing, my smile? How can my own body language get them to perceive the value I want to project—the value of my résumé, of my goals in life, of the product I'm working on, the product I manage, the raise I'm asking for, my next upward move?

We all do this all the time in our personal lives. Whatever the specific objective, we're all always putting forward who we are in order to achieve what we want. Think about casual day-to-day instances in which your nonverbal projection is making a statement: maybe the car you drive, the drink you ordered, how you stand at the bar, the way you answer emails, the picture you just posted. Every day our subconscious is selling us, and most of us don't know it and can't stop it! So while self-promotion sounds narcissistic and selfish, it makes more sense and makes life a lot easier to be aware of our self-promoting ways and to accept that, in many instances, it just comes naturally to us. The smart move, in fact, is to put that natural trait to work *authentically* to get you the career success you seek. Your body language has to project the differentiating value you can bring to a job. That value is communicated when you can correlate exactly who you are with the way you put yourself forward. Control your actions, read their reactions, and curate the value you have received from that reading to get noticed in the way you want.

Before a word is even spoken, your just-right preparation for presenting yourself virtually speaks loud and clear.

Take it from me: if you are selling a bullshit front that you think maybe someone wants to see even though it really isn't you, you, too, may end up having a full panic attack in the client's bathroom during a sales pitch. As I learned the hard way, there isn't a healthy longevity in selling yourself, nonverbally and verbally as well, in a manner that really just isn't you at the core.

By the way, all of this holds true in the virtual world as well. The COVID-19 pandemic made it abundantly clear. Neither Zoom, FaceTime, nor audio-only communication can keep you from acting and reacting authentically or from projecting yourself as well as you can. So, if you are hosting a call or a meeting, make sure that you have tested your Wi-Fi ahead of time, that your background setting is presentable and in tune with the purpose of the meeting, that you prepared a proper backlight so people can clearly see you, and that the computer audio is operational so they can hear you. Before a word is even spoken, your just-right preparation for presenting yourself virtually speaks loud and clear.

Putting Words to It: Owning Your Story, Then Telling It

When I said that controlling your verbals means writing your own script, I meant it literally. The writing process helps you pare down to the essentials and forces you to articulate the intrinsic meaning you're trying to get across. When professionals need to communicate verbally, they nearly always use prepared scripts. Comedians have planned their bits and rehearsed them over and over. Announcers know their opening lines, their monologues, their big moments. Political figures and hot shot chairmen of the board use autocue or teleprompters, and when they flub a word here or there, you wonder if they read the damned thing before they opened their mouths.

• • •

YOU, TOO, NEED to transfer what's in your brain onto a tangible document. Pen and paper, Word doc, Pages, whatever. And the key to writing your own verbal communication script is to know your story. So, with your planned restart in mind, write down your answers to these key questions:

- ⮌ Where have you been?
- ⮌ Why were you there?
- ⮌ What qualities of strength were required—and how well did you meet the requirement?
- ⮌ Where are you going next?
- ⮌ What differentiates you?
- ⮌ How has your past developed you to where you are today?
- ⮌ What weaknesses have become strengths?
- ⮌ What weaknesses are you still working on? What are your unique accomplishments?
- ⮌ In less than thirty seconds, why you?
- ⮌ What notable accomplishments have you achieved?

Answer those questions in a concise paragraph on a single piece of paper or in a note on your phone, and you have a differentiating biography you can use in any number of situations. Memorize it, lock it down, and carry it with you in your brain everywhere you go.

Back when I was preparing for consulting and banking interviews, there was, weirdly enough, a standard question often asked by interviewers at top-level companies: "How many Ping-Pong balls can fit into the overhead of a 747 aircraft?" At one level, this is a reasonably complex math question; you establish some metric of the size of a 747, figure out the total area of passenger space in a unit of measure you can further explain, correlate the passenger space to proposed overheard space, calculate the volume of a

Ping-Pong ball, and then, from the suggested information, derive a logical answer. But this question isn't asked to get an answer. Who really cares about the number of Ping-Pong balls in a 747? It's asked to see how the candidate thinks about a problem. Your story needs to show that as well: how you approach a problem, how your brain moves, how you work with others, how you go about putting together solutions, whether you carefully set an expectation of how much time you would need, how succinctly you can express verbally what's happening in your brain, and finally, how you make the solutions happen.

Not an easy task. It requires self-examination, a lot of thinking, and then the hard work of "writing" your answer. Believe me, as a first-time author, I can tell you that the writing process is damned hard. Figuring out how to say what you want to say is demanding; it can take draft after draft after draft, each with new ideas, new suggestions, then more ideas and more suggestions, and then another draft to get it to say what you really, truly mean. Oh wait, you need to add something, and then something else. Just one more draft!

But ideally, that's what you should do. First, determine the story you want to tell. Second, write it down. Third, tighten it up, target what you really mean, zero in on that, tighten it again, pare it down to its absolute essence, hone it till it's razor sharp—not just the whole story of you but also quick sound bites you can memorize easily and pull out of yourself when needed.

That's why I'm recommending you break the story you want to tell into a minimum of five power lines for every meeting or sales pitch or job interview or email to a recruiter, not to mention to every first date or, hell, even your appearance on *The Bachelor* or *The Bachelorette*. You know what I mean by "power line." We've all seen TV shows where a government official or business leader or actor or musician is being "interviewed," and what we hear in the seconds or minutes allotted is a quick, succinct, articulate, powerful message the individual is determined to get across. That didn't come out of thin air. It was proposed, prepared—possibly by a committee—shaped, drafted, redrafted, and polished till it shone. On every show I have been on from *The Today Show* to *Good Morning America*, *Yahoo Finance*, *Celebrity Family Feud*, and even to *Bachelor* premieres and finales, every television personality, while talking, is listening to an earpiece telling them to move the show faster; any and every guest has only seconds to make an impact.

Take a similar approach in creating your five power lines. First, make sure each is something you really want to say, something that aligns authentically with you at the core. How can you be sure that works? Talk to yourself about it. Try each power line out. Identify the one you think is the clearest, that says what you really mean and says it short and fast. As one of my wittiest and funniest friends, Roby Farchione, references: "Brevity is the soul of wit"—Shakespeare.

For me, I go through these tryouts—then rehearse the ones I choose while taking a shower, while driving, while waiting for the morning cup of coffee to be just right. Why the shower? It's probably the one place in the world where I don't have any distractions. No television, internet, people, dogs, phone, computer, books, nothing except for me, soap, and hot water. I can bloviate to my heart's content till I find the power line that works.

But that's just me. You'll easily find your own best place or circumstance for rehearsing your power line. Time it. Tighten it. When it's taut enough, sharp enough, and feels good in your mouth, it's right. Let it become second nature, ready to pour out of you with ease either when the opportunity strikes or when you're backed into the corner.

Few things are as valuable to a professional as the ability to tell a story succinctly, from start to finish, while keeping an audience engaged, whether you're making a speech in a huge conference center or delivering a power line one-on-one. It is a skill set that involves both art and science, and it will have a material impact on your restart. I know that not everybody is at ease with public communication. So here's an exercise I've used when refining the basic verbal communication skill set. It, too, works well in the shower and is effective in making you even more comfortable with the sound of your own voice and with your ability to find the right words.

Imagine you're telling a second grader how to make a peanut butter and jelly sandwich. Go step by step: the types of PB, the contest between smooth and chunky and the arguments put forth by proponents of each; the flavors of jelly; the bread choices. How to open the jars, what utensils to use, how to spread each element. Slice off the crust? Yes or no. Cut on the diagonal? The range of opinions on that issue can be wide. Narrow it down.

You may ask yourself why I am asking you to assume that your audience is a second grader. Two reasons: First, with the numerous distractions and given the speed of technology, today's adult population has the attention span of a second grader. Second, we always assume people know what we are talking about. They don't, not any more than a second grader would. Assuming you're talking to a kid in second grade requires you to supply all needed details—as briefly and as fast as possible. That's great training for keeping your verbal communication on point and on time.

Also, as you talk to yourself, listen to yourself. Vary your inflection and watch your timing. Learn to pause, to vary your tone, to stop when the point has been made. If you're providing an explanation, start at the beginning and finish at the end. Be precise but snappy enough to hold the attention of that second grader.

Does this sound like a lot of work? Does it sound bizarre? It can be an essential part of the productive planning process and a solid way to strengthen your attention to every detail of the all-important first impression. Remember that your aim is to sell the person who will succeed in the new career you are looking for—the person you now understand yourself to be, ready for a fresh start in a career that aligns with your new definition of success.

Simply put, planning, preparing, and rehearsing/practicing well ahead of any in-person presentation can fortify your ability to project the differentiating value that will be the hallmark of your restart.

All the Shit That's Fit to Stick

- ↯ For your restart, you aren't selling a product or service; you're selling your new understanding of who you are and of what constitutes success in your eyes.
- ↯ Uncomfortable or intimidated by the prospect of selling yourself? Get over it. The fact is that every second of every day you are selling and being sold to.
- ↯ Two elements of marketing are at work in any self-presentation: the nonverbal and the verbal. Both are potent marketing mechanisms and will serve as essential sales tools.
- ↯ We all know that you never get a second chance to make a first impression. But the truth is that you only get seconds to make the first impression to begin with—and making the right first impression is absolutely imperative.
- ↯ Know your story and how to tell it. Your story needs to show how you approach a problem, how you work with others, how succinctly you can express verbally what's happening in your brain, and how you make the solutions happen.

8

Eliminating the "Work" from Networking!

*N*etworking!

I know. We have heard the word a thousand times over; most of us know we should do it, usually avoid it, and get annoyed thinking about it. You picture yourself sticking a name tag on your chest and approaching a room full of people you don't know and who don't know you, but who seem to know one another very well. It's a scenario terrifying enough to almost disable some people. In fact, I learned from a consultant the bank brought in to lecture us on the subject that open networking is the third worst fear we all have—just a bit down from death, which gets top billing in the fear universe, with public speaking in second place.

It shouldn't be so terrifying. When you get right down to it, all networking is, technically, is meeting people you don't know, which is something we have all done all our lives. But finding and following the connections among those people we don't know presents each of us with a puzzle. As with any puzzle, we have to find the right pieces, and of course put them in the right places, so we can get to where we want to be. It's all about finding that next piece to keep the puzzle moving along toward completion.

Networking is the heart of it, so here is a hack you can implement immediately. It has helped me become a better interviewer, especially when big-time guests who intimidate me come onto my *Trading Secrets* podcast. The hack is: just be genuinely curious. Think through what you genuinely want to know and fill any empty space with a thought-provoking question about the individual. Listen to the answer and reengage with another thought-provoking question. Everyone loves to talk about themselves, and everyone is impressed by those who are attentive to their story. It's a simple hack, but it can raise the relationship-building success rate in your networking efforts.

And where restarting your life and career is concerned, networking is absolutely essential. You already know, but what I'll do in this chapter is reframe how to think about networking, then show you how to do it and how to make it work for you.

Let's start by realizing how well equipped you are at this point to actually be networking like that one guy or gal you know who does it best. You've done a lot of self-examination and have arrived at a significant level of self-understanding. You've looked inside yourself and identified the superpower within you, the essential characteristic that differentiates you and on which you will build your brand.

The beauty of that brand is that it's transferable throughout your lifetime for the obvious reason that it is *inside* you, so you carry it wherever you go. Unlike that company you work for, the title they gave you, or the boss who gives you your annual rating, your brand lives within you, which is why it lives on. No one can take it from you; it travels with you anywhere and everywhere you go! As morbid as it sounds, your brand may even live beyond you. It is your legacy, and your legacy can be infinite. I think about my grandpa who passed: I could write another book just on his story and his brand. It is your brand that lives forever, not your title, not your company, not your job. If you're asked what your purpose is, point to your brand!

Right now, after all the reframing and rethinking you have done, it is your most important asset for getting you the change you want. But part of driving that change lies in finding the right people to help you along the way.

And inevitably, you will need other people. There isn't one successful individual in any industry who has achieved success without the help of others. Not one! Think of someone you look up to. Now think of the product you may buy from that person, or the blog or book that person wrote, or the content they put in front of you. That person has an army behind them, a full team helping them. In fact, it is the team behind the people you admire or want to emulate that is usually one of the driving differentiators in how and why you distinguish them from their competition.

Now, think about you, your network, your eventual team. You have identified your brand, but you will now need to connect with others who can direct you to opportunities, assets, actions, and yet more people. Yes, you're a free agent looking for a new deal that will lift you out of where you are now, and you've got a great brand to "sell." But you still need the phone number or personal email of the decision maker who can say yes to what you're offering. And for that you need the contact info of the person who knows the decision maker. More likely than not, it will take a few more zigzagging connections to reach *that* person as well. Patience and strategy: you need both to find the next piece of that puzzle that will get you to the next connection you need.

That's why networking is actually the greatest shortcut there is to success. I know some people look down on the whole idea of taking shortcuts, but my feeling is if a shortcut is legal and ethical, I will take it every damn day of the year. These days, everyone has an angle, and not all of them are entirely ethical. I have seen it at every stage of my life. In college, every sports team, fraternity, and sorority had test files dating back ten-plus years, saved in the hope that professors never changed the questions, and so kept handy for students. And then the students from those organizations would trade the tests like it was a drug transaction. In the corporate world, I have seen people steal leads, lie directly to clients, and even expense their groceries on their business expense account. And in the entertainment world, holy hell! That's next-level-up fooling around with ethics. I could write a book just about that. Lies on lies on lies, PR stunts to cover those lies, settled cash-out agreements, gag orders, cutting someone off at the knees to get ahead—I could go on forever—and maybe I will! But my point is: find the angles, take shortcuts, but if you're in it for the long game, as you should be, do it the right way, ethically and legally! Otherwise, you are bound to get caught, and the margin for error when building that personal brand is razor thin!

And here's the question: How else are people who can influence the decisions that will affect your life and livelihood ever going to know you exist, what you're aiming for, and how you may instill value if you don't find your way to the people who know the way to those decision makers?

The good news is that if you ever leave your job, your title and paycheck will be gone, but the network you built will be as transferable as your brand: once you know people, you know them—as long as you stay connected in some way. Remember when I told you I wanted you to be a LinkedIn warrior? It's absolutely imperative for networking and therefore for bolstering your brand. In fact, your LinkedIn connections are your scorecard for your networking. What I mean by that is that for any connections you have with others—any interactions at all—you should damn well make sure you're connected with them on the most powerful business-networking tool out there, LinkedIn. So, if you find yourself a free agent again, if you get caught in what I got caught in—the bank in a hurry to get me back after my stint on

The Bachelorette, then making use of the five minutes of celebrity I gained there, then pushing me out as fast as possible when it was convenient—you still have your brand *and* your network.

You can start right now by simply searching for people who went to your high school or college who may have some tangential connection to the company or industry you're trying to get into. There is an unmatched alma mater camaraderie that causes people to almost always want to help others who share that experience.

In addition, join the industry networking groups on LinkedIn. Look for "power users" with large networks and consistent content posting that generates discussions and comments. Respond to someone's comment; use their content as a means of discussion to ask for an introduction to someone in their network. Individuals have built careers—some have even built empires—relying on this specific networking strategy.

I hear you. You're taking this in, but it doesn't lessen your reluctance to go up to a total stranger at a conference, to send a blind email, or to make a phone call to someone you've never met.

That's fine, because that is not the kind of networking I am advocating. Not at all.

Networking: Something for Something. How *I* Hire People!

I'm not asking you to go Wolf-of-Wall-Street-cold-call-style to pick up the phone and start dialing. What I mean when I say *networking* is much more like precurrency barter. When one of our ancestors some eight to ten thousand years ago killed a huge *Sivatherium* (a cross between an antelope and a giraffe) and, after feeding his family, had plenty left over, he might just swap a chunk of those leftovers to a hungry friend of his—preferably one who was particularly good at sharpening whatever instrument our ancestor had used to kill the *Sivatherium* in the first place. To swap food for assurance that the food-preparation instrument stays sharp and effective certainly constitutes an exchange. A good of a particular value is being exchanged for a service of reciprocal value; that is a win for both individuals—and for their families! The exchange doesn't even have to be immediately reciprocal, but the reciprocity is understood: you did something for me today, and I will do something of equal value for you when you need it.

Everyone you come across is a potential networking possibility, and both of you know this inherently, so it isn't even mentioned.

Our hunting ancestor understood instinctively that the key to the exchange was to offer value before asking for it—in his case, showing the hunk of meat being offered and only then suggesting the sharpening expertise he sought in return. That's the core of networking; it's the way to get it started. Ten thousand years ago they had it figured out, and we still struggle to understand and execute this simple action called "networking."

And guess what? Just as with selling, the truth is that we're all doing precisely that kind of networking all of the time. Everyone you come across is a potential networking possibility, and both of you know this inherently, so it isn't even mentioned. And each of you is ready and available to consider an exchange of favors that can benefit you both.

The perfect model of networking to study is friendship, specifically the friendship formed when you are part of a team. I think particularly of sports teams primarily because I played on teams all my life but also because friendship during a sports contest is so absolutely immediate. It's a brotherhood, a kinship. You have each other's backs. You can count on each other totally and every minute. That's networking at its very best.

I grew up watching *Survivor* religiously, and on the first night of *The Bachelorette*, I was already looking for my allies: the people I could trust, at least for the seventy-five days or so I was in the *Bachelorette* bubble. I found them: Wills, Grocery Store Joe, Colton Underwood, Blake Horstmann, and Garrett Yrigoyen. The six of us "clicked" right from the outset. We would sneak away, ruffle our mics so the producers couldn't listen to our conversation, talk about things going on in the production, and try various tricks to help one another. And as it turned out, four of us were in the final four, one ended up winning *The Bachelorette*, one became the next Bachelor, one became the main character of *Bachelor in Paradise*, and one became a huge hit on *Dancing with the Stars*. But these relationships built early on saved me on the show, after the show, and still to this day.

We had each other's backs, we helped each other through the process, took pains to find out more than we were supposed to know, and looked out for one another once filming started.

You are the sum of those you surround yourself with, so be selective. Make sure there is a balance of value and that you have friends and colleagues that make you a better person. To have great friendships, you must be a great friend, and that exchange of value goes for personal and professional relationships as well. Having a strong relationship with a decision maker will put you in a better position to win.

Networking literally goes all the way back to your preschool. As children we start becoming friends with other children, sharing toys with some of them in exchange for their toys, their companionship. This lives through us in all stages of childhood schooling. Who we become friends with, sit with at lunch, participate with in camps, dance classes, sports teams, everything. We network naturally the minute we begin communicating. As grown-ups, as professionals, we just as naturally keep reengineering the process, gravitating to what comes easiest in building relationships with people we don't know but who may matter to us and our goals.

It seems to me that there is a possibility of networking around every corner. I had the chance to go to the 2021 Super Bowl thanks to a couple of friends who belonged to the same country club as one of the owners of the Tampa Bay Buccaneers (one instance of networking). Meanwhile, during halftime, a young man came up to me, said he recognized me from *The Bachelorette*, loved *Restart*, was a follower, and asked if I would take a photo with him. Of course I was flattered and pleased to do so. I liked his forthrightness.

Later, we went to the Bucs' after-party, which, thanks to the connection with one of the owners, we got invited to despite being Bills fans. In the middle of the party, who comes up to me but the same young man who had asked for the photo! This time, he rattled off a list of qualifications and ambitions, then politely but eagerly asked if he could apply for a summer internship with my company!

We did some vetting, and yes, he could and did come and work with us that summer; among his numerous qualifications for the internship, he certainly had expertise in networking. Evidence of that expertise? He knew that the key to it was to offer something of value *before* he asked for value in return. In addition, the moment he felt I was impressed with his credibility, he was quick to execute and ask for a favor in return. I have found that anyone who has ended up working with me has a similar story. Kaity McGee landed a job by sending me a pitch email. She had researched my brand and took YouTube thumbnails that I had been using and made them better through her own creativity. In return she asked if she could do a few pieces of work for free for us. She demonstrated value, executed value, offered a free trial, and became a valued worker in my company!

Then there's the story of the worst deal I ever did following *The Bachelorette*. A guy named Evan Sahr approached me to do an appearance at a New York bar called the Ainsworth. It would pay me a fee of $500, the least I had ever been offered, and it would not pay for my travel from Seattle. I declined. So Sahr asked me if I might be "planning to come to New York any time soon."

"Actually," I said, "I'm coming this weekend to visit my brother." So Sahr got busy. By the time he had put it all together, he had me making appearances at two other bars on Friday and Saturday night, for substantial appearance fees plus travel expenses paid, with a finale at the Ainsworth on Sunday afternoon. The gig I had said no to turned out to be a highly profitable weekend for me, and it left me with an impression of Sahr as a kind of genius who got his way, got a win for me on what was a terrific weekend, and got others to pay for it all just by networking, negotiating, and selling. To this day, the pay I got from Evan ranks lowest of any compensation I ever had, while every other deal that he orchestrated for me that weekend paid big-time. So it was a great weekend for me and a highly profitable one for Evan. Talk about a win-win!

Evan Sahr is now a business partner with me, and here's the thing: whenever I meet someone for the first time, I put the person's name in my phone, never to be touched or changed. But Evan Sahr is still listed in my contacts as Evan Ainsworth!

The Value of the Referral

Yes, networking is so natural we do it all the time without being aware of it. Still, natural or not, it's also true that when we meet anyone for the first time—whether it's when dating or in business or in any other area of life—our guard goes up.

Someone you can't identify slides into your social media Direct Messages, the old DMs, or you get a random email, or a person you've never seen in your life shows up at your front door canvassing for a candidate or a cause: our instinctive reaction is to be wary. This could be a threat. It feels a bit intimidating. Our defenses are up.

That's why cold introductions of any kind are so problematic: the outcome of a successful networking interaction is very low when you show up unknown and unannounced. That natural wariness, the threat someone new represents, doesn't instantly disappear after a second or two. The person sliding into your DMs, the cold text, blind email, random front-door knock-knock-knock or, even worse, the cold-call phone call is almost never effective. Yes, there are some people who just have a natural gift for going up to total strangers in person, in an email, or on the phone—and cold-call networking, like the young man at the Super Bowl party, Zach Blank, who got the internship with me. If you're one of these people and you have that natural ability, keep killing it. Most people don't. So, for us, cold introductions are almost always unsuccessful. Again, it's because we don't *naturally* trust people we encounter at random. When we do encounter them, we tend not to allow our guards to come down; we simply want the people gone as soon as humanly possible. Which likely leads to hanging up the phone or immediately hitting the big red ignore button, not responding to the cold email, to messages, to a knock on the door.

But all of that can be avoided through the warmth of an introduction, by providing an intermediary who can turn the unknown into someone familiar. Even just slightly familiar. When someone you know and trust introduces a person to you, that's not just a link, a phone number, or email address; it's a seal of approval on that someone. So when it comes to networking your way into a career move, when someone known to and trusted by a person you have targeted refers *you* to the target, it's a seal of approval on you. The threat disappears, the sense of misgiving evaporates, the wall and the guards come down, and you become someone who belongs in the space occupied by the person making the referral and the person you're trying to get to. Thanks to that intro, there is now the likelihood of a relationship—no cold or blind communication is wanted or needed.

Having a referral doesn't mean you can forget about offering the something you have to give for the something you want to get *before* you make your request. Just the opposite: it makes it even more important to do it and to do it right. But the beauty of having a referral is an opportunity to personalize your "offer" of the service you want to provide, aligned as closely as possible to the needs of the person you're contacting. Whoever is making the referral for you is certainly doing you a favor, but probe him or her for help in framing your offer just right. That's the great value of the person making the referral: he or she knows both you and the person the referral targets. It helps you tailor how you describe the value you believe you can provide to the target *before* you ask for what you'd like to get.

Requesting a Referral: Research First

Where do you find people who provide you with referrals to targets you want to reach? Simple. Just do research. Actually, the people who can introduce you to the people you need to get to are right there in that natural network of contacts made from preschool to the current moment. You just have to find the connections, and that may take a number of steps. Somebody you know knows somebody who knows somebody who knows somebody else. It's basic, but it works if you actually put it into practice. Know those you're connected with and know those they're connected with. The line between you and the contact you have targeted may twist and turn, and it may seem long, but hang in there. Step by step, it will get you where you want to go.

It's easy to say it's all there on your phone, but hell, it's true. Nothing is more powerful for gaining information and connecting the dots of your contacts than social media. That's why you need to spend whatever time it takes to systematically probe all your platforms for all the contacts you can find. You will discover connections you never dreamed existed. Then, just as systematically, ask connection A for a referral to target 1. And keep going till you score. You know about six degrees of separation, right? These days, with social media, I genuinely believe it's four or five degrees. It's never been easier to find people to connect with. You *will* find people who know people who know other people who can get you to the person you want to get to!

One important recommendation as you search your contacts, your social media, your friends and family, and anyone else you can find as "candidates" for your networking: diversity rocks. This is a lesson I learned in business school, not in class or from a textbook but rather in the way the school selected our teams before we started class. And this team was my ride-or-die for the two and a half years it took to complete my MBA.

The team selection process was based on detailed tests we had to take on entering the business school. Supposedly the tests analyzed our personalities and capabilities. The aim was to make each team as diverse as possible. No two team members should share much more than the ability to speak English. All of us on my team came from different places, had different backgrounds, studied different subjects in college, and were different in personality, skill set, thought process, and just about everything else.

The team was amazingly effective, precisely because of those differences. We each brought our own individual dimensions to the team activities that were the fundamental structure of our education: the way we thought, the way we analyzed situations, the way we framed and articulated our presentations and discussions. The bottom line was that our wildly different strengths made us a hell of a team, and wildly different strengths can make a hell of a network for you as well. So look for contacts who come from different backgrounds and ways of life, who think differently, who represent different fields, hold different jobs, are in different trades, possess different talents. That kind of diversity can help your business, your career, and you yourself grow.

Research, Request, and Now: The Response!

If there's only one thing you take away from this chapter, let it be the three Rs: research, request, and respond. Those three Rs will change your life. But for now, there you are at last, getting to the person you want to get to, poised to connect personally with him or her by phone, email, in person, whatever. Your strategy now is simple: again, offer what you've got to trade *before* you present your ask. (If the person making the referral could hint beforehand at the value you have to trade, that's even better.) As a guy who wasted a thousand dollars of the bank's money on taking people out to lunch to build relationships, I am telling you: don't follow that classic standard. Be more strategic and create some real value. First of all, lunch in a restaurant is actually a transparent financial gift. Second, the individual you're trying to win over eats lunch every day and can probably afford a meal without your help. A lunch offer is not going to sound to him or her like it provides any particularly useful advantage. Third, there's nothing differentiating about it. Anyone can expense a meal in a restaurant. Instead, do something meaningful, do something that differentiates you.

> *As a guy who wasted a thousand dollars of the bank's money on taking people out to lunch . . . I am telling you: don't follow that classic standard.*

What is that meaningful, differentiating something? Extend an offer to perform or provide the service that you believe creates value for the person and will therefore be worth an exchange. Maybe it's something that assists the person in doing his job, or an introduction to someone she wants to meet, or a marketing idea that the person's company hasn't tried, or an expertise that you believe would add value to the enterprise the person runs.

Networking Checklist

ONE, FIND YOUR niche—the unique value you can bring to others.

Two, identify your targets.

Three, do the research!

Four, request the introduction.

Five, respond by figuring out the best forum for making your pitch—from a coffee "date" to audio notes to requesting a private interview.

Six, remember that you are not asking for a favor; you are suggesting a trade—and you are making your offer of the value you can deliver before you ask for anything in return.

Seven, create the pitch—how you will deliver that distinctive value that can extend the person's reach and ignite a snowballing effect of ongoing value for you both.

Eight, package it, deliver it, network it wider.

And remember the three Rs: research, request, respond!

Okay, I am now throwing shit at the wall and hoping that one example will stick! But the point is to customize a differentiated and thoughtful way to add value that cannot be replicated by "just anyone." As best you can, make it a service, an action, a customized, targeted *something* that you are uniquely positioned to offer, something that exemplifies a particular strength, talent, or advantage that only you can bring to this person. Remember, all that's needed is for each of you to need or want what the other has, then for both of you to make the exchange.

I'll give you an example. I was thankful for my time on *The Bachelorette* and met a big unscripted executive at ABC that I really liked. I remember him telling me he was a huge New England Patriots fan, so the next time I saw my childhood friend who happened to be the tight end of the Patriots at the time, I asked him to sign a mini helmet I bought for forty dollars and to make it out to Rob Mills. And for the cost of forty dollars plus shipping, Rob Mills got a Patriots helmet signed by Gronk.

When I left *The Bachelorette*, I saw that the products that veterans of the franchise were offered in sponsorship deals were pretty much all of a piece. They were hair products, health products, fitness products, and beauty and fashion products. I saw them all as just so many toothbrushes—everyday items that we all use. As I analyzed it, I saw that anyone coming off *The Bachelor* franchise could automatically get a gig selling toothbrushes.

But there was nothing differentiating, either about these toothbrushes or about the audience the sponsorships reached. Therefore, as I saw it, my rate for sponsoring a toothbrush was never going to be higher than the rate offered to any other franchise veteran who commanded a larger and/or more engaging audience.

Surely I could provide something that would differentiate me from the others. Yes, many of the franchise veterans had business backgrounds more or less like mine, but there were aspects of mine that were unique: I had an MBA in accounting and finance; I had spent ten years as a corporate banker; I had executed more than $150 million in deals, had relocated all over the country, had achieved the success I had hoped for only to find that it made me miserable. Once I created a brand around my uniqueness, I attracted a whole different kind of client: Credit Karma, State Farm Insurance, H&R Block, QuickBooks. I was even hired to speak to every incoming Capital One intern across the country.

I had now built a brand that was a niche, and as a result I attracted sponsorships from national business and finance-focused companies and have ownership in a financial-tech trading app.

This in turn enabled me to create my own business networking group, my own business podcast—*Trading Secrets*—and the social media community *Restart*, which creates more than a million impressions a week.

I attracted business-branding companies, and I even had ownership in my own financial technology app.

The lesson is clear. Develop your own differentiating brand and make *that* the value you offer in exchange for the service you seek. Be the unique supply to fill a demand your contact might not even realize he or she needs. That's a value that rates way above taking that contact to lunch.

Sometimes what you're offering will be immediately accepted and the return request immediately reciprocated. That's a quick exchange that can benefit both parties at once. But it doesn't always work that way. Sometimes you'll get what you came for while the person giving you what you want holds your IOU, and you never quite know when you'll be asked to make good on it. (Just make sure you do.) Going above and beyond for those asking for guidance will pay massive dividends in your credibility, good will, and Karma. Building a network is a long-term investment that can last a lifetime, so it is essential to be deliberate and exercise patience.

I honestly believe that your network *is* your net worth. And more important, I am convinced that it is a predictor of what the rest of your life will look like. That is certainly true in my case. What makes me think so? For one thing, you wouldn't be reading this book if it weren't for networking and the platform it created. How do I know that? Because I wouldn't be writing this book if it weren't for my networking, which led me to the show, which led me to building a financial consulting business, which led me to an agent, who introduced me to the HarperCollins Leadership group! In fact, my experience with networking offers an almost textbook example of why it isn't a matter of what you know but who you know, as I'll explain next.

Building a Platform

So I come out of this wacky, wonderful, kind of amazing experience of being on ten episodes of a reality TV show until I finally got dumped in the middle of Thailand. And I dutifully return to the bank to make good on the agreement we made. I resume my banking duties *and* take on additional duties that sort of exploit my fifteen minutes of fame until suddenly and summarily, I got pushed out.

Now what?

Ten episodes of a very popular TV show, as it turns out, endows an individual with something of a brand. I'm *known* in a particular way. If I add ten years of banking expertise, lending more than $150 million, an MBA in accounting and finance, plus a number of cohosting and guest appearances on other shows, that boosts my reality TV brand. It becomes an odd combination of business and entertainment, selling and communicating, each energizing the other to create a platform that I think is unique to the worlds of both business/finance and of entertainment/celebrity. That was a good move. In a big space, it effectively differentiated both me and my platform.

Then the COVID-19 pandemic hit, and economies around the world went ballistic. Every day brought another headline about the Dow and the S&P sinking fast. In fact, the S&P alone dropped 34 percent in twenty-three days, down from the peak level reached on February 19, 2020. Not long afterward, on March 10, 2020, the Dow lost 10 percent in a single day, its worst drop since the historic 1987 "Black Monday" crash, when it collapsed by more than 22 percent.

How close were we to a total stock market bust? All anybody could do was to keep watching the Dow and the S&P—and to pray.

That gave me an idea. Not the praying but the bit about watching those two key stock market indexes. I'm a banker/investor/business owner with an MBA; I look at the Dow and the S&P

every day the same way I breathe. But I suddenly wondered whether the huge numbers of people now clueing into these two indexes really understood what they were looking at. I wondered particularly about an important segment of the population: women ages eighteen to forty-four who make up the majority of my "audience."

So I put out a poll via my website asking my followers to define what the Dow Jones and the S&P were. I got more than 250,000 responses. More than 91 percent of the people responding gave the same answer: they had absolutely no idea what the Dow Jones was, absolutely no idea about the S&P 500.

To me, this was outrageously eye opening. Yes, I was kind of stunned at the gap the poll revealed between what we're taught and what we know. But mostly, I saw a way that I could provide value at least to the 91 percent who couldn't define the Dow and to anybody else who might find my platform. I knew I had a particular ability to explain financial issues such as credit, capital, debt, banks, taxes, mortgages, allocating assets, building net worth—basically anything and everything having to do with money. And I knew I could explain it in terms of real-life scenarios that would make sense to my particular, demographically defined followers. I also knew that doing so could and would empower and benefit them.

For the Dow and the S&P, the real-life scenario I compared them to was the first thing that happens to you when you go to your doctor or find yourself in an emergency room: the vitals check. Somebody takes your temperature, checks your pulse, measures your rate of breathing, encircles your arm with a strap, and computes your blood pressure. Taken together, these vital measures offer an indicator of your overall health, a quick look at the body's vital organs. The measures demonstrate either that you're basically fine or they alert the medical staff that something may be wrong. They don't delve deep or explain; they just measure and provide an indicator.

That is exactly what the Dow and the S&P are: indicators. Both are useful in telling us how two bunches of stocks traded on US exchanges are performing, not why they are performing that way.

That presentation clicked. It hit a nerve, and the "explanation" went viral.

This told me I had found a niche that brought a unique value to a significant and thriving demographic. A niche that I alone could occupy.

Now the question was how to build on that to create more value for more people by expanding what the brand signified and by extending its reach. I started by creating my *Restart* Instagram page, then created a YouTube show, and I asked the people to whom I had explained the Dow and S&P to come follow me there. My aim was simple: I wanted to generate more clients, enter into more advertising and brand deals, and gain more prospects while also offering free and impactful value to those who followed.

That worked. I got the clients, the deals, the prospects. So I was doing well in terms of numbers and growth. Time to expand to the next level and add deeper, richer value.

I decided the way to do that was to add interview guests to the mix via my YouTube and *Trading Secrets* podcast shows and/or just go live with them on Instagram. But how does a guy known for being on a reality TV dating show get to the big-time movers and shakers in the business world? How could I reach the very people I wanted as my interview guests? How could reality-TV-me make a persuasive networking pitch to people like Jim Cramer, seen by millions daily on *Mad Money*; or Kevin O'Leary, aka "Mr. Wonderful" from *Shark Tank*; or Ryan Serhant from *Million Dollar Listing*; or GaryVee, the CEO of VaynerMedia; or Dana White, who created the UFC—the Ultimate Fighting Championship? These were the giants I thought could really bring something special to my audience, if I could get them to speak the language I knew my audience could hear. But what unique advantage could I offer such giants in exchange for their guest appearance? I figured I had better do some research to try to figure that out.

To say I was surprised by what my research showed is an understatement: I learned that at the time I asked, I had nearly the same or a higher number of followers than some of my guests. Certainly not up there with the monster followings of GaryVee and Dana White. These are big personalities, and all very well known. They're innovative, brilliant, and experienced; and they make important statements regularly to vast TV audiences. But apparently, in the business community, even monster stars don't always get the same followings as a reality TV dating show contestant.

And that's how I built my pitch. I would offer them added value that only I could provide—specifically, access to my particular audience. And as you can imagine, our overlapping audiences are drastically different. But in addition, we would create even more value together through the "something new" we would represent, thanks to the compounding effect of our combination. The pitch started with me establishing both credibility and familiarity by referring to my business education and to my ten years as a corporate banker who loaned a lot of money and did well for my employer. In other words, I was telling them I spoke their language. But I went on to say, "My platform is really the reality TV universe, which means that thanks to the following I gained on reality TV, I can promote your brand and businesses on my platform." Then I quantified with detailed analytics.

The bottom line for the guests I wanted to invite on my show? Entry into a unique and powerful niche in the market that could boost their own brands significantly.

It worked. For both the guests and for me. All benefited from the unique value that being on my show brought them. For me, the move catapulted me to more than a hundred thousand followers of *Restart* Instagram, brought me a podcast deal called *Trading Secrets*, a YouTube show, an exclusive *Restart* networking group, ownership in a fintech app, a weekly newsletter, merchandise sales, business brand deals, and an offer to write the book you're reading right now.

It all came from the process of networking and doing it with a differentiated purpose.

Some of the Guests on My YouTube & Podcast	
• Jim Cramer	Leslie Mosier & Rob
• The Bella Twins	Chianelli
• Shawn Johnson &	• Dean Unglert
Andrew East	• Elena Davies
• Daymond John	• Patti Stanger
• Barbara Corcoran	• Zac Clark
• Kevin O'Leary	• Lo VonRumpf
• Peter Weber & Kelley	• Dr. Paul Frank
Flanagan	• Chicks in the Office
• Tyler Cameron	• Lewis Howes
• Lauryn Bosstick	• Rob Dyrdek
• Chef Anne Burrell	• Hugh Henne
• Ryan Serhant	• Harry Jowsey
• Chrishell Stause	• Gary Vaynerchuk
• Erika Nardini	• Pinky Cole
• Dana White	• Girl with No Job
• Hayley Paige	aka Claudia Oshry
• Josh Ostrovsky	• Corinne Kaplan
(The Fat Jewish)	• Marc Lore
• Anthony Pompliano	• Nick Viall
• Johnny Bananas	• Tilman Fertitta
• Paul Bissonnette,	• Anne Heche &
aka Biz Nasty	Heather Duffy
• Doug the Pug Owners,	• Joe Amabile

CHAPTER 8 RESTART REVIEW

All the Shit That's Fit to Stick

↻ Unlike that company you work for, the title they gave you, or the boss who gives you your annual rating, your brand lives within you, which is why it lives on. It's your most important asset for getting you the change you want. But part of driving that change lies in finding the right people to help you along the way. That means you've got to network.

↻ Nervous about networking? Remember, there isn't one successful individual in any industry who has achieved success without the help of others.

↻ Networking is the shortest path to success, and if you think taking shortcuts is wrong, think again. If a shortcut is legal and ethical, take it!

↻ The network you build is as transferable as your brand. Once you know people, you know them—as long as you stay connected in some way.

↻ The perfect model of networking to study is friendship, specifically the friendship formed when you are part of a team.

9

Let's Get You Paid!

Gamifying the Negotiating Process

*I*t's time to talk about money.

I don't mean a conversation between you and me; I mean it's time for the world at large to talk about money.

Back in the days of officially stratified societies, the lords and ladies who had all the wealth decided that "money" was not a fit topic for conversation—certainly not in polite society, where etiquette was what separated those lords and ladies from the rest of us.

Thankfully, those days are long gone. But that bit of etiquette around silence on the subject of money got baked into the blueprint we all grew up on and survives to this day. We already know that only 37 percent of us ever even ask for a raise; the other 63 percent find it simply too uncomfortable to deal with.

It's insane. These are discussions likely under ten minutes that can change our entire future. And yet we can't deal with the discomfort? Turn on any form of television, and you can hear everyone from celebrities to people's grandparents discussing their sex lives. But money, of all things, is still a taboo subject.

Well, it simply cannot be taboo when you are going after a job or a raise, so let's all grow up and put away any squeamish notions about using euphemisms or finding a "polite" way to ask for the job, salary, benefits, vacation time, bonuses, title, responsibility, profit sharing, expense account, housing allowance, and anything else we are asking for because we believe we are worth it. Let's instead be honest and candid about two simple facts of life: what we pay and what we are paid.

After all, if we can't talk about these things, we can't measure them. And if we can't measure them, how will we ever know our value? For, in the world of work and business, value is measured in money, right? Money is the scorecard, and getting the value we deserve is what negotiation is all about.

"Money Talks"—Time to Talk Back

The first step in negotiating occurs long before you get into the room or on the call to make your case to the person who actually "decides" your compensation package. It's a simple step: Know your worth. Know how to justify that worth. And identify your monetary value through research.

The more information you can extract, the better off you will be in this process. Start by gathering all the information you can about that value judgment both inside and outside your company. For the tasks you perform and the benefits your performance brings to the organization, what *can* your company pay? What do other companies pay, and what is the market paying for work of equal substance and value? Those figures constitute the baseline of any negotiation. Any one of them can hamstring the decision maker with whom you are negotiating and advance the case you are making.

How to find the numbers? Begin by exploring the available "public" knowledge—the facts about pay grades and salary ranges and performance review schedules, both in your company's policy handbook or human resource guidelines and in the policy handbook or HR guidelines of every other company you may research. Chances are you will find a lot of talk about "ranges" from minimum to maximum, about "levels" of compensation, and about "scale." But no actual dollar figures.

With that as a general framework, you're positioned to at least start asking questions about actual numbers. Does this mean going up to a colleague and asking what her annual salary is? Yes! That is precisely what it means. The only way to get comfortable talking about money is to start talking about it. Eventually, someone will respond in kind. And for those who don't? Ask yourself why. It's likely because the place of employment doesn't condone it. Why not? Because it provides you more information that can ensure that you are paid appropriately! So, yes, ask your colleagues; in fact, the key place to start is right there, in your very own network of colleagues and coworkers. Then keep going. Ask around in your extended network of people as well to learn the value placed on other kinds of work that may be relevant to yours.

Does this mean going up to a colleague and asking what her annual salary is? Yes! That is precisely what it means.

Remember the *Chicks in the Office* podcast? Fran and Ria? The company they work for is Barstool Sports, which has an advanced way of thinking about compensation: for one thing, people who work there are quite open about how much they make. And imagine this, the two cohosts go into performance reviews and negotiations together! It's not a secretive operation where one complains "against" the other: Fran gets this, but Ria only gets this and vice versa! Fran and Ria make exactly the same amount in compensation: same dollar amount, same bonus splits, same total package. Since they *cohost* their podcast, negotiate as one, and fully understand the calculation and equation of what value they add, this makes sense. It also makes sense that they negotiate together because they know that it is their joint work that makes the show a success; they know that they both put in the same amount of work and carry equal weight. When each does well, the show does well, and both do well. And while Barstool certainly has its critics, everyone should commend them for the forward-thinking way they see the value in employees by creating transparent and open communication on how their coworkers are compensated.

But don't stop at asking your coworkers how much they make. There are people all over any company who know the numbers. The people in the HR department see the numbers all the time. Ask some forthright questions of staff there—especially the recruiting staff. Look to outside recruiters as well; these are people who structure and submit job offers all day every day.

The internal finance department is another place where people know the numbers. So do executives who head teams. So does the vendor management group that negotiates the contracts for any outside services the company uses.

Yes, look at the websites of companies that do the work yours does, and explore economic analyses by trusted online sources. You want to try to get beyond the standard but elusive discussions about job grade, level, and range to actual numbers that express the value of the work being done—the benefit that your work brings to your organization, the advantage you provide by doing the work the way you do it. You're trying to measure that value as clearly as possible so that you can negotiate on the basis of how much value you add, to make your numbers higher. This is an essential step toward growing your own wealth over time.

Confidence that the price tag you put on your value really does reflect your value is essential to negotiating successfully. Just be sure you really do know what constitutes your value and what doesn't. I very nearly slipped up on this shortly after I came off *The Bachelorette*, when I was asked to go on *Bachelor in Paradise*. This show, which films for some thirty to forty days, is universally known to be a total shit show. All previous cast members from all the shows in the *Bachelor* franchise come together on an island and see if they can date one another. It's wild, it's crazy, and some folks think it's tacky, so I definitely wanted my stint on it to be worth it.

My first negotiation was to ask for a higher daily rate than the $300 that was being offered. I negotiated that up to $600 per day. But there was another factor involved: what if the bank fired me because I was participating in something wild, crazy, and tacky? This was a far cry from when I went on *The Bachelorette* with the bank's permission *and* to its eventual profit. So, while I had won a higher daily rate, I also wanted a guarantee from the producers. What I negotiated was a commitment of $5,000 from them. So, even if I was sent packing the first day, I would at least be paid $5,000.

Sounds good, right? Wrong. There is short-term or stopgap value, and there is long-term value. I realized that the value I had gained from *The Bachelorette*—the brand power it brought specifically to me—came from being authentically me on the show. To engage in the *Bachelor in Paradise*'s shenanigans and to turn myself into a goof suddenly seemed like a move that could diminish the brand I had won through *The Bachelorette*. Not a good move, I realized, to increase my value. Rather, this might tarnish it a bit. And my intentions weren't very authentic this time around. My only real aim in going on *Paradise* was to be on TV again. I wasn't ready to go find a life partner just weeks after getting dumped on Season 14 of *The Bachelorette*. So I bowed out of the "deal" I had struck and never went on the show at all.

What the Hell *Is* Negotiating, Anyway?

The word *negotiate* has at least three dictionary meanings: to work out an "arrangement" through talk and discussion, to get past an obstacle (you want to "negotiate" that slab of ice on the sidewalk *very* carefully), and to make a bargain. You'll need to do all of that in negotiating, whether it's for a raise or a new job or a transfer to the company's Honolulu branch or to the Buffalo branch (each to their own). And you will find that after you get past any obstacles, the bargain you arrange is in fact an exchange of value. That is the heart and soul of negotiating: both "sides" benefit in some way, or there's no deal. And if a deal is struck in which there is *not* benefit to both sides, the one-sidedness will in time be exposed, and any longevity for the deal will be lost.

A few paragraphs ago, I used the word *hamstring* to describe the power that facts can bring to your negotiating stance. I hope that didn't suggest that you should equate heading into a negotiation with going into battle. In fact, that is absolutely the wrong way to proceed. Again, negotiating is about both sides succeeding, each getting *something* so as to create a win-win situation. If you have a chip on your shoulder, leave it at home when you negotiate; this is a discussion between consenting, mutually respectful humans, not a contest in "toughness" or in outlasting the opposition.

But there's something even more basic to negotiating. It's really about emotions. When you meet with your boss to negotiate for a raise, you will succeed only when you get to his or her emotional center. What excites this person? What is he or she afraid of? If you can connect emotionally with the decision maker's enthusiasm and fears, you are likely to get what you came for. "An ounce of emotion is worth a pound of reason."

MTV desperately wanted to sign Rob Dyrdek. He knew the network wanted and needed him because of the ratings he was providing them. In negotiating a new show deal with management, Dyrdek, in his own words, "went from making a $125,000 per-episode fee to taking in millions." How? He accepted the per-episode fee but also negotiated equity of integration rights. "So," says Rob, "I went from $125K per episode to millions per episode because I owned the platform." Understand the emotions of the person across the negotiating table, and your gains will surprise you.

I once heard a successful negotiator say that "it's not just that everybody takes something home from it. It's that everybody *feels* like they are taking something home from it." Emotion is the core of it, and making everyone involved feel like the solution arrived at was *their* undertaking is imperative.

It has long been known that emotions affect decision making. Rational decisions made on the basis of expected utility are invariably influenced by the decision maker's emotions at the exact moment of decision. And as we all know, emotional states drastically change by the hour, by the day, and by whatever stage of our life we're in. Research on this subject began in the latter part of the last century and continues to this day. Besides, we all know it's true because we know that our emotions affect our decisions. The important thing is to be aware of that.

Being aware of it when you are the one seeking a decision that will help you means looking for what excites your decision maker and what makes him or her uncomfortable or afraid. Reinforce the former and avoid the latter, and you help your chances of getting a favorable decision.

How to create that connection? I look to two practitioners who excel at it: really effective interviewers like criminal investigators or exceptionally sharp journalists, and cereal boxes on a supermarket shelf. I'll explain.

Obviously, a criminal investigator interviewing a murder suspect is dealing with someone he or she believes has already stepped outside the norms of social behavior. That means that normal social tactics are not going to work with such an individual, so the investigator might mirror the suspect's body language, position his or her questions in a preposterous order, or act out a kind of gonzo bond with the suspect. The investigator knows that the suspect will only confess when his or her emotions are so affected that all logic is gone. He or she has to "play" the suspect on an emotional basis to get the confession needed.

Back in 2003, ABC's *Primetime* featured an interview by Diane Sawyer with Britney Spears; it was later the subject of a documentary titled *Framing Britney Spears,* which tells you just how upset Spears fans were by the *Primetime* interview. Sawyer's voice never rose above normal volume as she asked a series of questions, probed more deeply into some of the answers, and raised issues already widely exposed in public. Calm, gentle, intelligent, modulating her voice from classically cool to concerned and sympathetic, Sawyer staged an interview that not only zeroed in instantly on the young star's emotional core but also opened her up. If you watch the interview, you can see how Sawyer makes it happen: the pauses, the waiting, the steady, seemingly caring serenity that gets past all the logic and makes the story a succession of emotional strings being played. Britney fans were outraged at their star's revelations and demanded that Sawyer apologize. The journalist and former news anchor never responded.

Now, most of us are not criminal investigators or distinguished journalists and crack interviewers, but the idea is the same. Get past the logic of your case to the emotions to which the decision maker responds. It's not about breaking anyone down; it's about winning the decision you seek.

This doesn't mean you don't need all the facts. On the contrary, exactitude is essential in the story you tell. But within the exact story about what you bring to the table and why it is worth what you're asking for, there must be a path to the decision maker's emotional center.

What does this have to do with cereal boxes? They can't talk, and frankly, the act of buying a box of cereal involves very little emotional attachment. But in fact, what that box looks like, its color and design, its price point, where and how it is shelved, everything about it has been carefully arranged to *negotiate with you,* the completely detached buyer. Along an extended supermarket aisle, hundreds of different cereals are *all* negotiating with you—first, for your attention and, once you've given that much, for your interest and then for your buying decision. The only way a box of cereal can do that is by reaching you emotionally, and cereal manufacturers spend an exorbitant amount of time, effort, and money aiming right for your amygdala, the almond-shaped portion of your brain where emotion is experienced.

For some of us, it could be the color of the box that does it. For others, it's the price. For some (kids most likely, but I have fallen for it in my thirties), it's because there's a prize inside it, or a contest on the back of the box, or it's a healthy start to the day. In the Kroger chain of markets, there's even a strategic labeling mechanism right there on the shelf that can tell you more about the product. I know this, because a company I have ownership in, Evoke Healthy Foods, pays Kroger thousands of dollars to place this labeling. In other words, something about an utterly emotion-free box of cereal reaches you in an emotional way, and that's the one you buy. I hope I didn't just ruin your view of those pieces of cinnamon toast crunch cereal that stare out at you with eyes and mouth wide open on the General Mills Cinnamon Toast Crunch boxes!

Put the two things together—the criminal investigating/crack interviewing and your buying decision in a supermarket aisle—correlate that with the research that has told you who is paying what to whom, and you have the basis of a strong negotiating stance.

Now correlate the criminal investigating/crack interviewing/ buying decision in a supermarket aisle with the research that told you who is paying what to whom, and you have the basis of a strong negotiating stance. You could actually create a T-chart of the two "variations" as a guide to getting to the emotional center of your decision maker.

Of course, to do any of that, you need to understand the emotional center of that individual, and to do *that*, you need to put yourself in his or her shoes as best you can. Once you're there, you can attempt the same kind of third-degree probe of priorities that you gave yourself back in chapter four, digging into what moves and motivates this individual, what creates fear or worry in him or her, and what drives him or her to excitement both within the workplace and in personal terms.

Actually, you already know a lot more about this than you think. One way or the other, you have watched your decision maker in action for some time and with more than normal interest. If you have observed carefully (and we do tend to observe our bosses pretty carefully), you should be able to analyze their successes and to understand what may have made them fail. You certainly know what they think of you. You understand how your work or position has affected their life and career, and you undoubtedly have a good idea of what drives their decisions.

Stop and think about the times you've seen your decision maker enthusiastic about something. Look back over the interactions between the two of you to recall times you've seen a bit of worry on their face. From your own observations, you know your decision maker's principles, style, what drives them, what makes their life difficult, the future they are looking for.

Let's say that you knew that your decision maker's decision maker, the head of the division, had expressed her "disappointment" that the team hadn't "generated more revenue" over the last quarter. Sure, everybody knew that. After all, few institutions on earth are bigger rumor mills than a corporate workplace. But not everybody will know how to use that information. It's a safe bet that your decision maker will be focusing enthusiastically on productivity in the coming months while worrying about the numbers. Boom! Right there, you now have a lot of emotion-focused information.

Apply your T-chart of the two emotion-seeking variants— investigation plus cereal box—to what you already know, put yourself in your decision maker's shoes, and you will realize that you already know what excites and what scares that decision maker. Build your negotiating "ask" around arousing both of those emotions, and make sure the value you bring to the table touches that emotional center as well.

The Art of Negotiating

By the way, I do believe that the impulse to negotiate is universal. In me, it is so automatic as to almost be subconscious. I do it all the time.

I also appreciate a master negotiator when I see one, and no one is more masterful in negotiating, positioning, and selling than the Bachelor Nation star Colton Underwood. Talk about playing to the emotions of the decision maker *and* of his audience! Colton does this better than anybody I have ever seen, and it seems to come naturally to him. You probably know that getting cast into the lead role of *The Bachelor* requires a number of interviews. Colton and Blake Horstmann and I have talked to one another about our interviews, which, for Blake and me, were pretty vanilla and straightforward. The interviewers asked us questions about ourselves, and Blake and I talked about who we were and what we wanted our vision to be for what was next.

Colton went into that interview prepared to sell to these powerful and experienced masters of television the thing he believed they wanted with all their heart, which was not necessarily what *he* wanted. As he later told me, he "looked into their eyes," agreed with them that Blake and I were good guys, "guys I want to have a drink with," said Colton. "But do you want good guys, or do you want a good TV show that gets you ratings, because *I* am the guy who will deliver that."

Spoiler alert! As you already know, he got the gig, and he was right: a twenty-six-year-old former NFL player, stunningly handsome, head of a nonprofit, and a virgin looking for someone to date and possibly marry. It made for great television. Since then, as most know, Colton has come forward very publicly and announced that he is gay. I am happy for him for living his truth and coming out. It is beautiful. I am incredibly proud of anyone who speaks their truth, and I am a strong supporter of The Trevor Project. I urge you, the reader, to visit thetrevorproject.org to understand its mission and perhaps support this incredible cause.

But back to business and *The Bachelorette*. Colton also wrote a book that was published just as the COVID-19 pandemic was locking down the country in early 2020. In fact, he himself became ill with COVID early on; he was certainly the first from Bachelor Nation to contract the awful virus. At this time, there were no book tours for publicizing a new title and no bookstores where buyers could browse. Everything was closed. But Colton talked very publicly about the disease he had endured, informing listeners about its physical and emotional toll. While fortunately he recovered well, he also gained national attention from all the COVID coverage—right at the pinnacle of his book launch. Boom! His existing platform, brand, truth telling, and highly entertaining story had his book soaring off the shelves at a rate authors like me can only dream of! Crushed sales, a very successful launch, and a *New York Times* bestseller! Colton crushes it again.

He always told me that he has long wanted his own show, and he positioned himself thoughtfully and carefully to get one. He actually asked me to do a casting call for a show he and his one-time girlfriend Cassie Randolph were planning. Inevitably, that fell through after they broke up, and he pitched me on possibly doing another show with him, one where his other friends and I were his wingmen in his new dating life. That, too, fell through. But when Colton has a vision, it's remarkable how it always becomes a reality. As I write this, multiple reputable sources are saying Colton has been filming a show for Netflix centered on the story of his coming out, months before his exclusive, one-on-one with Robin Roberts on *Good Morning America*, where he officially came out publicly. A powerful story and one that is bound to be as impactful and as winning as the man himself.

But the takeaway from his example is to do your positioning, planning, and strategizing *before* the selling. Then watch the results work in your favor.

Planning 1: Establish Your Value, Name Your Price, Set a Date

Every new job starts with a negotiation, and it is essential in that first negotiation that you hold out for as high a starting salary as you can. Why? Because that starting salary becomes the baseline for every raise you will ask for or be offered over your career in that company. It also becomes the baseline when you leave that company and try to move to another. Increasingly, hiring managers demand to know what your starting salary was at the company you're *leaving*. It means that even a thousand-dollar difference in starting salary in your next negotiation can make a difference that will impact you throughout the entirety of your career.

This is just one reason why planning is essential when you negotiate. Well ahead of entering into a negotiation, you must plan every aspect of it thoroughly and precisely, or risk failure. By "every aspect," I do mean from soup to nuts: from setting a date for the meeting to "scripting" your way into your decision maker's emotional center while not sounding scripted at all.

Moreover, recording all of your planning on paper, on your device, in whatever way makes you comfortable, is absolutely essential. Draft your notes however you like, save them, refer to them, tighten and improve what they tell you, review them, hold on to them, and preserve them.

The first preparatory step of planning is to define your goal. Specifically, your money goal. Whether for a raise in your current job or for a whole new job in a whole new organization, what exactly are you aiming for in setting out to negotiate, and how might your decision maker respond? The two questions are inextricably linked, because unless you can show that you will be delivering value equal to the value you're asking for, your decision maker will have little reason to grant what you ask.

You've already determined several of the elements that are likely to go into the process of defining your money goal: you know where your current total package stands in relation to what your organization can pay, what other organizations pay for equal work, and what the market pays for equal work. Add to this mix the value of your historical performance in this or any other organization, the value you expect to add when you get what you're asking for, and the cost of replacing you (or, if it's a job negotiation, of not hiring you). Then quantify the value you expect to deliver to your decision maker. All of these are valid and legitimate components of establishing a money goal.

Now, in an in-depth memo to yourself, define your value to the organization, the wider corporation, and the decision maker. This definition should cover these points at least:

- What objective deliverables have you been a part of or do you execute regularly? What is the financial value of those deliverables in terms of added revenues or costs saved? What nonfinancial benefits have those deliverables achieved?
- What special projects have you managed or executed within the organization? What has been the revenue or savings impact of those projects?
- What is the value of your work output divided by the cost to achieve that output? What are the capabilities you bring to that equation—among them perhaps your creativity, the speed with which your output is achieved, your education, your connections, your ability to drive the business?
- What specific advantage(s) to the organization could not have been realized (or in a new organization will not have a chance to be realized) without your particular skills,

connections, or abilities? Identify those particulars and quantify the revenue and/or savings of those advantages.

- What would be the opportunity costs of your *not* being part of the organization? Measure these costs in terms of the time and resources that would be needed to replace you, the loss of your deep familiarity and comfort with organizational processes, the loss of the sheer speed of your output, the loss of your education and skills, your possible recruitment by a competitor organization.
- Identify your leverage within and outside the organization: What is the demand for what you do? What is the supply both within and outside the organization to fill that demand? What is the added-value "bonus" you bring to your work? Maybe the speed at completing a task, or your unique creativity, your connections outside the organization, your singular talent for communicating? What might be the cost in time, productivity, and operational effectiveness of having to meet the organization's demand for a replacement?
- Given your record thus far, what is your value inside the organization and, equally, outside it?

Quantify the answers to all these questions. Think of the memo that contains the answers as the equivalent of the cereal box that sells itself to customers. Bring to their attention all the details about you that are "on the box": your brand, your uniqueness, your proven capabilities, your measured achievements all proving your particular worth to the organization. Like the carefully designed, carefully placed cereal box, this memo establishes to a T what your value is and what you should be paid for it. This time you're Cap'n Crunch, and the decision maker is the consumer strolling among the boxes of cereal.

So now, put a price tag on what the memo shows you are worth. Then, my advice is to add 15 percent and make *that* your negotiating goal. In addition, set the dollar-figure bar below which you won't go. You will want to establish that bar early in the negotiating process, as we will see, so be very sure of the number you set. That number should be derived from all of the previous investigating you have done.

Also, get as much vacation time as you can. The reason? Paid time off accrues and therefore likely will be paid out in the event you leave. Think about it: if you get an annual four-week vacation, that's the equivalent of twenty weekdays for which you have to be paid. If you then decide to leave the job, you would get those twenty days of salary at your departure—a nice buffer that could tide you over when it's time to restart.

If you're nervous, that's normal.

Next, create a formal calendar invitation for a set date and time and ask for a face-to-face meeting, either in-person or virtually, so that you can read the decision maker's reactions and see how your message is being received.

At this point, you're ready to prepare your negotiating argument. And guess what. If you're nervous, that's normal. It's all good! Sometimes, even showing your nervousness can create the human element that drives emotions.

Planning 2:
Preparing the Emotional Argument

You've already figured out what creates fear and excitement in your decision maker, and you now know the precise value and leverage you bring to the organization. The aim now is to position the latter to drive the former. It's time to present yourself as an individual who can put to rest the decision maker's fears while simultaneously meeting the expectations of his or her enthusiasm. That's why you're worth what you're asking, and it's why the decision maker will win when you do.

Suppose your decision maker is due to retire in three years. You know this woman; you know her priorities; you're certain that what she wants is to finish accomplishing the long-term goals you've heard her talk about before she leaves the organization. How can you position your value and leverage in a way that shows her you are prepared to help her do just that? You see what is most important to her, you share her intense desire to make it happen, and you have the will. You also have experience in the organization, a unique creativity, and above all the proven project management skills to get it done right, in return for the raise you seek. That can surely drive a decision maker's emotion to create a win-win for the two of you.

A different example: your decision maker has shepherded your group through two tough years of mediocre performance, and everyone knows he is worried about keeping his job. You know that, in addition, he has just bought a new dual console boat for fishing, and between that and the mortgage on his fairly new house, money is precious. Your value for reducing his fear lies in your people management skills, your knowledge of the ins and outs of the organization, and your cost-cutting record. These skills will help him keep his job and his paycheck. Your leverage is that you understand his fear and are ready to go to work to put it to rest. In exchange for your ask, you both come out on top.

That is why negotiating is really all about emotion. It's time to bring some emotion into your negotiation planning.

Planning 3: The Details

Once you are sure you have identified all the moving parts in your planning—the full package of information and argument—you're ready to prepare yourself for the actual negotiating session.

Start with the room where it happens. If it is to be an in-person meeting, it will most likely take place in your decision maker's office or conference room. He or she will choose the setting. Chances are you have been there before, so you know the entrances and exits, what the furniture is like, how the place feels. If you're negotiating with a new organization, at least check out their annual report photos or website or other PR visualizations so you can at least get an idea of the design style you may be confronting. As best you can, feel comfortable about being there.

If this is a virtual negotiation, ensure ahead of time that you have the appropriate Wi-Fi strength, that your background is dignified, that the lighting works. Get private: you really don't want roommates, dogs, or small children bursting in on you or being heard through the door.

Then, define what will be most comfortable for you to lean on during the face-to-face session. Perhaps you would prefer to send a pre-meeting written memo to your decision maker that outlines the points you will make: your value, the leverage you bring to the table, your carefully worded statement of understanding about how your value and leverage connect to the decision maker's needs, and the outcome you are seeking.

Some people are comfortable with a pitch deck that lays out their argument and its reasoning in concise, attention-getting visuals. Or perhaps you're more comfortable with your notes consolidated into as simple an outline as you can create, which you then memorize till you can recite the points in your sleep. Whatever crutch you find most comfortable, most reliable, and easiest to deal with, prepare it well ahead of time. Practice using it, and of course remember to bring it with you.

Be sure all the facts on which you will base your case, your argument, and your ask are at hand—either in your head, in the pre-memo, or in your pitch deck. Getting what you came for will depend on your comfort in discussing plainly and openly that most uncomfortable of subjects: money. It is the facts you've uncovered in your research that are the real strength of your argument.

Then rehearse the session in your mind. If you can, practice it out loud to yourself and/or to others till you feel comfortable expressing what you are asking for.

You can help yourself feel *physically* comfortable through planning as well, and it's certainly worth doing. I asked for some tips on this important subject from Shawn Johnson, onetime gold-medal Olympian gymnast and later a winner of *Dancing with the Stars.* Shawn knows precisely how to control her body and keep it working for her. Her suggestion? Visualize your "performance."

In training for the Olympics, she told me in an interview, "the last thing you can think about is that you're at the Olympics and it's the biggest stage in the world." That doesn't help; in fact, it actually creates self-doubt that can lead to mistakes. Instead, repeatedly visualizing herself *executing the routine as if she were in her home gym* is what brought her the gold. In essence, she was "keeping the blinders on" until the competition was over. Trying to picture an endpoint takes your focus off your performance, especially if that endpoint is perfection.

If you can put yourself in a Shawn Johnson–like zone through prior visualization that pushes out the negative, then the things you visualize have a good chance of coming true. It's all about planning and getting your head focused well ahead of time.

Here's a story about pre-preparation that I owe to Jennifer Aniston, a woman I have long admired. Besides finding her absolutely wonderful looking, she has always struck me as incredibly likeable. She's a genuine person who connects with people directly and in a way that puts them at ease. I saw her in person for the first time at the *E! People's Choice Awards* in 2020. In fact, I was seated quite close to the podium but, due to the shape of the room, was actually behind it. So, in a sense, I saw mostly the backs of the speakers. My seating, however, gave me a little insight into how Aniston achieves that effortless naturalness. Three massive monitors contained not just every word she uttered but every pause, every directional signal to turn her head left, right, or center, every breath to take. This genuine, from-the-heart speech had been planned, written, timed, utterly pre-prepared in every detail. That did not make it less genuine. Not at all. It just showed how absolutely imperative planning is. This is someone who acts and memorizes lines better than almost anyone. And she still put all her lines and every detail of her appearance on a teleprompter!

Practice your "power poses," take in box-breathing strategies developed and executed by Navy SEALS, get leveled, focused, and ready to go. Plan and be prepared. Every time, without fail.

In the Room

Wherever the "room" is—even outdoors or on Zoom with a fake background—you and your decision maker are there to negotiate. If you can, begin by setting a tone that diminishes any discomfort either of you may feel. A good way to get yourself into that tone is to think about someone you admire. Chances are the person is not a jerk, not a bully, not someone who leaves a bad impression or comes off as threatening. On the contrary, the odds are that a person you admire is not just admirable but also likeable, and likeability is an extremely good way to establish the right atmosphere for negotiating.

Of course, composure is key, yet staying calm and in control of yourself and your responses can be tough. A few years ago, I was traveling in Europe with my ex-girlfriend, her brother, and an older friend of mine (actually my high school hockey coach). At one point during the trip, it was just Coach Tom and me on a train to the Berlin airport to catch a plane to Paris. We were just approaching the airport station when two men wearing matching jackets with some sort of impressive-looking logo entered the train car, asked the woman sitting next to me for her ticket, stamped it, and then turned to us. These were physically impos-ing guys; they clearly "outsized" my retirement-age coach and skinny me, both of us loaded down with backpacks and cases. "Tickets, please," one of them said, just as the train was coming to a stop in the station. Having rushed for the train, we hadn't had time to buy tickets—nor did we need to. So we got off the train and started walking toward the airport.

The imposing-looking guys followed us. "You will need to pay a fee for that," one guy said, "in euros, cash only, no card." If we hadn't guessed it before, it was now clear that this was a scam aimed precisely at unsuspecting tourists in a hurry and carrying too much luggage.

"No ticket, so you pay right now," the guy went on, looking big-ger and sounding even more threatening. We were at the far end of a long concrete walkway to the airport, with no one else around.

Coach and I quickly assessed this shakedown. The two big guys clearly had the physical advantage, and the woman with the "ticket" had also clearly been part of the scam. We understood that for us to respond in a threatening way would achieve nothing good. And we also understood that our main goal was to catch the damn flight to Paris.

"Here's what's going to happen," I said to the three. "We travel with cards, so all that we have in cash is fifty euros. You take the fifty euros, and we will pick up our bags and continue to the air-port to catch our plane. If we pass a policeman on the way, we will continue walking. This never happened."

They took the deal and got what they wanted: our cash. For get-ting taken, I guess you could say we got what we wanted in return, given the circumstances: an escape from physical harm and a walk to the airport for our flight. We managed it by maintaining our cool and by keeping our real goal in mind as we negotiated the best "win" for both sides. Composure is key. Try hard to hold on to it.

At the same time, be very clear in your mind about what your goal is in this negotiation. Know precisely what you want in quantitative terms. Be specific about why you deserve what you're asking for. Remember also that you are aiming at your decision maker's emotional center, trying to align what you want with what he or she wants, offering value for value. Stay positive and in control of yourself as you make your case. Remember that it is a very strong case. Here's how to put it out there:

Demonstrate your value by enumerating the qualitative and quantitative benefits you bring to your decision maker. This is the base of your "offer." Expand on it by outlining the argument you have created that is aimed at the decision maker's emotional center, stirring that individual's enthusiasm or fears. Make clear that you know precisely what you have committed to deliver and let your decision maker know how you will deliver it. Remind him or her how the exchange you're asking for brings equal value to both of you.

Then make your ask for an equal exchange of value rendered in whatever quantitative terms you have chosen, such as a raise, benefits, better health care insurance, tuition reimbursement, vacation time, or profit sharing.

Be aware that in this and every negotiation, there will be a race to setting the expectation, and that is a race that you need to win. Put that expectation out there before your decision maker or whoever else on the other side even has a chance to tell you that "there is a range." Beat them to it with a built-in set of expectations. They may have a range, but you have a bar you won't go below; the two are incompatible. Only by setting the expectation bar first can you make your price the standard around which both sides are negotiating.

Quantify your leverage for the decision maker and be aware that it includes all sorts of values you can bring to bear. Stack your leverage with a degree achieved, a personal talent, your creativity, your history, statements of support or testimonials, all of which can be advantageous to your decision maker. These are the selling points that can drive your decision maker's emotions.

Be clear that leverage also includes the willingness to walk away, but keep in mind that there are two types of walking away. There is the absolute walking away you do when your minimum ask is rejected, and there is the walking-away-to-think-further-about-the-counteroffer that has been presented.

Watch the body language of your decision maker and others. If they are ruffling papers or fiddling with their phone or if their eyes are blinking, those are signs of possible frustration or boredom. It is time to move on.

By the same token, be aware of your own body language and adjust it as needed to reflect your determination, your seriousness, and your likeability.

By the way, I would be remiss if I didn't mention that not everybody agrees with me about the power of likeability. I remember a lecture back in business school by an ace private equity expert. Private equity guys are often equated with killer sharks, but they are also known to be great negotiators. The lecturer began by asking us students what should be done to a ship full of attorneys that is sinking out in the middle of the ocean. We had no idea. "Let it sink!" thundered the private equity guy. "If anyone ever tries to control your negotiation, you will get worked!" He then advised us to create every possible discomfort for the "other side": demand an early meeting in your own office, then show up late, turn up the heat (literally), don't offer water, make everyone as miserable as possible.

It is certainly an opposing view, and I do not recommend it. As our mothers taught us, you catch more flies with honey than with vinegar. But the idea of not letting anyone else take charge of your negotiation—*especially* a private equity guy—is sound.

Stay in control of yourself, your goals, and your negotiation.

Make your argument, state the ask, then be quiet and listen.

The moment you are given any positive reinforcement that your ask is being considered or granted, stop talking. Don't oversell it.

When you have achieved what you came for, acknowledge it, and bring your participation to a polite end.

If you do not achieve what you came for, do the same: acknowledge and stay gracious before you walk away. The truth is that the world is full of other opportunities available to you.

CHAPTER 9 RESTART REVIEW

All the Shit That's Fit to Stick

- ⚡ Money is still a taboo subject. It's time for that to change, especially when you want a job or a raise. So let's grow up and learn to have those conversations.
- ⚡ Before you negotiate for a job, a raise, or anything, it's critical that you know your worth and measure it in monetary value.
- ⚡ Knowing what your company and others pay—and what they *can* pay—requires research, and you'll be surprised at how much you can learn online by looking at public documents.
- ⚡ Keep in mind the words of a successful negotiator: "It's not just that everybody takes something home from it. It's that everybody feels like they are taking something home from it."
- ⚡ Be clear in your mind about what your goal is in a negotiation. Know precisely what you want in quantitative terms. Be specific about why you deserve what you're asking for.

10

Restart, Rewire, Reset Right Now

The people we admire the most in this world almost surely fell on their faces a hundred times over before they became the people who now arouse our respect, our applause, and maybe our envy. Press them in an interview, as I have occasionally been able to do, and they all have a story about how they screwed up big-time before they found the path to becoming who they are today. In every single case, *something* ignited a restart in their lives. What got them where they are in the world is that they took hold of that something and ran with it.

The trick, of course, is to know that something—that restart catalyst—when you see it. But thanks to that tired old blueprint we all grew up with, spotting it the first time around isn't always easy.

Did you know that the first *Michelin Guide* was published in 1900? It included maps and instructions on how to change tires, which Michelin manufactured. In fact, the whole purpose of the guide was to get the French public off their bicycles and into cars, preferably riding on Michelin tires. So the guide also told readers where to find gas stations, and it added a list of hotels and restaurants. That simple profit motive for a tire company was the modest start of what has become the bible of haute cuisine, the standard to which great chefs aspire, and the world guide to fine dining everywhere. It sure didn't look that way in 1900; it set in motion a restart almost nobody could see.

I've told you just about everything about how long I trudged along without spotting my restart, even though it was pretty much staring me in the face. After all, seeing a shrink, popping beta-blockers, racing for the first drink at the end of the workweek, and suffering the Sunday Night Scaries should have been enough to propel me out of the life I was living and into something else in two or three or maybe five years. But ten years? My waste, but at least I am making up for it now.

I wish I could identify *your* restart catalyst for you, but I can't. That's beyond any author's powers, although I certainly hope that this book helps you to start looking for it. Making a restart in your career and your life requires that you break down walls, dig deep, get vulnerable. "There is no other way," I wrote back then, "to get out of where you are now and into where you really want to be."

You want to know what finally did propel me out of where I was and into where I wanted to be? It wasn't a financial disaster, a health scare, or a career mess-up. It was a failed relationship in my twenties. Who doesn't have a failed relationship in their twenties? But in this case, it was the girlfriend to whom I had given all of my trust, loyalty, and commitment. Not only that, but she broke up with me the day after we returned from what was a wonderful, fun-filled, joyous family celebration: my brother's wedding. She lived in Buffalo, and I lived about sixty miles away in Rochester. We flew from our respective towns and met in New York City for a wedding packed with friends from the Buffalo area as well as generations of family members.

Actually, I sensed that something was off that whole weekend. I even saw a text battle between my girlfriend and her brother in which he kind of scolded her about the way she was handling things. I wasn't sure what that was about until the day after we arrived home when I got the "we need to talk" text. We talked, and soon thereafter, she broke off the relationship. It took some time for me to connect all the pieces, but I learned that she had had a someone else while I was still her "something." Talk about a gut-punch!

The breakup absolutely knocked me off my feet. She had become so much a part of the path I was on, so essential to the picture I carried in my head of the success I would enjoy, the steady rise in position and title and money and success in that particular "ecosystem," and with all the trimmings. The breakup totally shattered that picture.

So it wasn't the obvious hint of trouble—the beta-blockers, the Sunday Night Scaries, the shrink—that set my restart in motion. As I said, I already knew that stuff had to end. It was obvious. What shook me to the core was realizing that the success I was working so hard to exemplify was a success defined by other people—by the girlfriend, by our friends, by our families, by our shared ecosystem. That realization hit me in a weird place. Maybe a bit of it was having "lost out" to another guy; male competitiveness can be funny that way. And maybe it was a bruise to my ego to discover that I wasn't quite good enough when I thought the image I was putting out there was of a guy who always exceeded expectations.

My bell had never been rung the way that breakup rang it, and it changed me. Suddenly, I could see clearly what I had always known deep down: I just didn't fit in that particular "success" ecosystem. It wasn't *me*. And I was exhausting myself trying to keep the fire burning in a life where "me" didn't fit and wasn't happy.

Looking back on it, the breakup was a blessing for both my ex-girlfriend and me, but for me personally, it was also a wake-up call, and what it said was, "Good morning, why are you doing what you are doing, and why are you doing it the way you're doing it?" Great questions, both of them. As I began to probe for answers, I found an awful lot of "stuff" in the way. I realized that any time anything had gone "wrong" in my life, I had found a protective mechanism or strategy that would make me feel better. As a result, I had built up a substantial supply of crutches, life jackets, and cushions to shield me from realizing what was going on. If I felt a panic attack coming on, I had pills to level me down. When the five days of career prison were over, I had the race to the bar to mark the moment by getting fairly blotto from alcohol. If I was "expected" to dress in a certain way and wear my hair in a certain style, I had a shrink who could calm me down after I complied.

The message I heard inside was saying, "Break the blueprint, Jason!"

I had to push those protections aside in order to get to the truth of me, and when I did, just like those people I mentioned at the beginning of this chapter, I fell flat on my face, good and hard. That was the catalyst to my restart. The walls were down, and I could finally see who I really was and what could make me happy.

Once I gave in to that, everything ticked in a whole new way. I felt different waking up in the morning, I worked out with less strain and more joy, I found myself searching my soul and liking what I found there, and I began mapping out a way to pursue my own interests rather than the bank's interest. I honestly felt my mind and body rewiring themselves, felt a new kind of power that put me in charge of myself. It's almost like the energy you feel when you fall in love, and it reminds me, when I think of it now, of the powerful blast of energy that falling in love with Kaitlyn triggered in me. It was like going from living in black and white to a hi-def life in brilliant technicolor.

When *you* find this new energy, hold on and enjoy the ride.

For me, that power is what made it possible to take the leap of faith to move to Seattle, knowing that the two-year commitment would provide me the financial freedom to lead my own life. It also gave me the chops to go on a damned reality TV show in the middle of that two-year commitment, a decision that not a single individual in my life—not a friend, not a coworker, not a family member—thought was a good idea. But by then I had stopped listening to others and was listening only to myself. The message I heard inside was saying, "Break the blueprint, Jason!"

So I did. It charged the power I needed to restart my career and my life the way *I* saw it, not anyone else.

Where Will You Go from Here?

You've been reading this book because you feel the need for change in your work and your life—a new beginning. As it happens, you couldn't have chosen a luckier moment for it. The world you and I live in is like the Wild West, a wide-open frontier where everything is changing, and every change is possible. It's true about the way we communicate, learn, work, play, find and build relationships, earn and spend money. "It is what it is" simply doesn't apply to this time in history.

That doesn't mean that change is easy; it almost never is. And where the kind of change this book focuses on is concerned, there are energies, systems, and factors that might slow the change down or burden it with difficulties. We've tracked and discussed a number of the difficulties that restarting a career in particular might present. But you know what they say about difficulties: the best way out of them is through them. Hard work and a state of discomfort are often prerequisites for meaningful growth.

The rock-bottom reality is that our generation, yours and mine, was born into a life expectancy of seventy-nine years. Break that down into growing up during the first eighteen years and living an adulthood of sixty-one years (give or take depending on factors outside the scope of this book). Why would you not live those sixty-one years your way? Why would you not live them in a way that brings you happiness and fulfillment every day of the week, every week of the year? Why would you not spend those sixty-one years living in a place you love, doing work you find stimulating, earning the pay you're worth and building the legacy you hope to leave? And hey! Why do we buy the cereal box that sells itself to us as we walk the supermarket aisle?

I hope that this book has both inspired and guided you, and I urge you, once you've closed it, to get out there and build your own road to wherever you want to go.

CHAPTER 10 RESTART REVIEW

All the Shit That's Fit to Stick

- Remember, making a restart in your career and your life requires that you break down walls, dig deep, and get vulnerable.

- The people we admire the most almost surely fell on their faces a hundred times before they became the people who now arouse our respect. They screwed up big-time before they found the path to becoming who they are today. In every single case, something ignited a restart in their lives.

- What will ignite your restart? I can't identify that for you. But if you do the work described in these pages, you will identify it yourself.

- If you feel the need for change in your work and your life, you couldn't have chosen a better moment for it. Everything is changing, and anything is possible. In short, it's a great time to break the blueprint!

- Wherever you decide to go, follow the map that *you drew* to get there.

ACKNOWLEDGMENTS

I said it earlier in this book, and I will repeat it right here, right now: behind every project, there is a massive team that delivers day in and day out to make the vision of that project a reality. Behind this book was an incredible team that worked to make my vision a reality.

First, I would like to thank my cowriter, Susanna Margolis, who worked endlessly to ensure she was capturing my true voice. While I know I can be a pain in the ass with countless last-minute changes, Susanna remained receptive and committed to making this the best possible book it could be! Thank you for your time, effort, and brilliant work! Thanks to my two test readers, Roby Farchione and Matthew Saccocio, who provided thoughtful and timely feedback. A huge thank-you to my friend and attorney Tyler Ellis for his expertise throughout this process. And to all of my close friends who consistently checked in on the status and process, you know exactly who you are. Gratitude and love to you all!

Evan Sahr and Julie Bortnick are the team that keeps the ideas flowing and the chains moving for the writing of this book—and for much else. Thanks!

To my agent, Courtney Paganelli, and to the whole team at Levine Greenberg Rostan Literary Agency, I will always be thankful. Courtney saw what I was aiming for, pitched the creative, and was absolutely essential in making this book a reality.

Likewise for the HarperCollins team—first and foremost editor Sara Kendrick for believing in the book's concept and taking me on, and also Louis Greenstein and David McNeill, the production group, and the marketing and publicity staff. I am grateful for your expertise and your efforts on my behalf.

Last but of course not least, I want to thank my family and partners in crime. Mom, Dad, Steven, Billy, and Kaitlyn, thank you for supporting me and always pushing me to be the best version of myself. Marcia, GL, and Liz, thank you for all of the love, guidance, and support. RIP, Grandpa T and Grandma T; I think about you two often. Sh-boom, Sh-boom . . . I love each of you more than anything in the world!

RESOURCES

SOURCES FOR COLA COMPARISON

CNN: https://money.cnn.com/calculator/pf/cost-of-living/index.html

NerdWallet Calculator: https://www.nerdwallet.com/cost-of-living
-calculator

SmartAsset Calculator: https://smartasset.com/mortgage/cost-of-living
-calculator

Bankrate Calculator: https://www.bankrate.com/calculators/savings
/moving-cost-of-living-calculator.aspx

Salary.com: https://www.salary.com/research/cost-of-living

NOTES

CHAPTER 2

1. Abigail Johnson Hess, "U.S. Student Debt Has Increased by More Than 100% over the Past 10 Years," CNBC, December 22, 2020, https://www .cnbc.com/2020/12/22/us-student-debt-has-increased-by-more-than -100percent-over-past-10-years.html.
2. "Facts," National Network of Depression Centers, www.nndc.org/facts.
3. "Provisional Number of Divorces and Annulments and rate: United States, 2000-2019," Centers for Disease Control and Prevention, May 4, 2021, https://www.cdc.gov/nchs/data/dvs/national-marriage-divorce -rates-00-19.pdf.
4. See note 3 above.
5. Dina Bass, "Bosses Are Clueless That Workers Are Miserable and Looking to Leave," Bloomberg, March 22, 2021, https://www.bloomberg.com /news/articles/2021-03-22/bosses-are-clueless-that-workers-are -miserable-and-looking-to-leave.

CHAPTER 4

1. https://www.nerdwallet.com/cost-of-living-calculator/compare /nashville-murfreesboro-tn-vs-new-york-manhattan-ny.
2. Nerdwallet's Cost of Living Calculator, www.nerdwallet.com/cost-of -living-calculator/compare/san-francisco-ca-vs-seattle-wa.

CHAPTER 6

1. "Labor Force Statistics from the Current Population Survey," U.S. Bureau of Labor Statistics, https://data.bls.gov/timeseries/LNS14000000 ?years_option=all_years.
2. The Enneagram is a system of personality typing that describes patterns in how people interpret the world and manage their emotions. The Enneagram describes nine personality types and maps each of these types on a nine-pointed diagram that helps to illustrate how the

types relate to one another. https://www.truity.com/enneagram/what
-is-enneagram.

CHAPTER 7

1. Kristi Hedges, "The Do-Over: How to Correct a Bad First Impression," *Forbes*, February 10, 2015, https://www.forbes.com/sites/work-in -progress/2015/02/10/the-do-over-how-to-correct-a-bad-first -impression/?sh=3bddb33355f6.

INDEX

ABOUT THE AUTHOR

JASON TARTICK is an entrepreneur, investor, public speaker, the host of Apple's top-charting business podcast, *Trading Secrets*, and a reality television personality. After about ten years in corporate banking, he took a detour into season 14 of *The Bachelorette* on ABC and has since followed that with appearances on *Good Morning America*, *Today*, CNN, Fox News, Yahoo, and *Entertainment Tonight*, among others. He is the founder of Red Ridge Consulting, a social media consulting company, Red Ridge Capital, a business lending and early stage investment company, and Restart, a company centered around career and personal money management. Jason's All Access Business Networking Group has inspired thousands to launch new careers and businesses.

Tartick's speaking engagements have ranged from talks at Capital One Headquarters to the New York Yankees front office, and have included many academic audiences at such institutions as NYU Stern School of Business, University of Kansas, DePaul University, Northeastern University, Loyola Marymount University, Iowa State University, and more.

Jason has made guest appearances on an array of television shows. Sparked by his time on television and his business endeavors, he boasts a social media following of more than 1.2 million. He and his fiancée, Kaitlyn Bristowe, starred together in Brett Kissel's music video, "Drink About Me," which received a Juno nomination. Jason was born in Buffalo, New York, but he and Kaitlyn now reside in Nashville with their two rescued golden retrievers, Ramen and Pinot.